Go *Love* Yourself

The Ultimate Guide to #liveyourbestlife

Heather Colleen Reinhardt

Published by:
HCR Media LLC
LOS ANGELES, CALIFORNIA
www.hcr-media.com

Copyright © 2019 Heather Reinhardt

ISBN (softcover): 978-1-7337403-5-7
ISBN (hardcover): 978-1-7337403-3-3
ISBN (ebook): 978-1-7337403-4-0

Editing: Heather Robibero and Mary Ellen Hettinger
Cover art: Candace Metzger • www.cjmetzger.com
Interior design: Gary A. Rosenberg • www.thebookcouple.com

Printed in the United States of America

"Love yourself first and everything else falls into line. You really have to love yourself to get anything done in this world."

—LUCILLE BALL

Contents

Acknowledgments

My mentor and dearest friend, David Norwood. Thank you for being the one who can see things more clearly when I can't (usually due to my Lakshmi weather pattern). Your wisdom and wit have supported me for the last 20 plus years. Gratitude doesn't even begin to cover it.

My best friend, Hunter Terpenny. The love and gratitude I have for you is impossible to measure. It's all happening.

Love, Mil

My family, Mom, Dad, Natalie, and Chloe. Thank you for loving me and supporting me when I "flew the coop." I wouldn't be who I am—or who I am becoming—without acknowledging where I came from. I love you.

My dearest friends, Heather Robibaro, Kiersten McIntire, and Elizabeth Maier. Thank you for being with me step by step, acting as my graceful doulas, helping me birth this self-love baby. I'm beyond blessed to have friends like you.

Glenda the Good Witch, Mildred Fizzbuckle. Where in the world would I be if you hadn't compassionately dragged me back to my yoga mat!? You are MY sunshine.

Love, Sunshine

My happy heart, Nathan Talei. Thank you for guiding me through my dreams.

Love, Petunia

The people who taught me self-care to the max, Mariel Hemingway and Bobby Williams. Thank you for the **#liveyourbestlife** lessons and mostly importantly, the laughs.

Love, Girl Friday

My forever soul friend, Jon Dadbin. Thank you for the lessons and the laughter. I never would have fallen in love with myself if you weren't a part of my journey.

The people I'm not actually blood-related to but I'm lucky enough to call family: Brittany Patterson, Nancy Lee, Noushin Talei Nikfarjam, and Sophie Nikfarjam.

My #highvibetribe: Adam Greenwald, Adam Krouse, Aida Lembo, Alicia Baker, Alyson Campbell, Amanda Cantrell, Andrew Roig, Anita Kabaei, Anna Reese, Ary Young, Ben Silver, Bobby Naderi, Breeanna Judy, Brett Hensley, Brian Canning, Brianna Burrows, Brittney Castro, Callie Jordan, Caroline Burckle, Catherine Neumann, Chevonne Hughes, Corrie Blissit, Dana Lieberman, Dana Bagley, Danny Rose, Deborah Ramaglia, Dena Benavidez, Diana Giovinazzo, Diana Lansleen, Donna Conrad, The Durrant's, Dylan DoVale, Eddie Finlay, Eddy Rimara, Ellie Hakim, Emily Gay, Emilie Perz, Erin Dunphy, Erin Sparks, Gabrielle St. Claire, Gilad Berkowitz, Haley Terpenny, Helen Vonderheide, Jarrell Hall, Jenna Macari, Jennifer Orellana, Jessica Bautista, Jessica Carroll, Joanie Eisinger, Joe Kara, John

Boddy, Jonelle Roman, Joy Sudduth, Kaela Crawford, Kare Morelli, Katie Jordan, Keisha Wright, Keith Leon, Keri Ports, Kimberly Keller, Kyle Biddy, Laine Ruscilli, Lorena Molfino, Lynne Sparks, Marni Gittleman, Matt Parker, Matt Richmond, Mia Togo, Mike Perry, Minling Chuang, Monica Caron, Nazanin Nour, Nikki Griffin, Rachel Newcomer, Rebecca Underdown, Robert Kazandjian, Rose Hilario, Ryan Seaman, Sarah Ezrin, Shayna Fischer, The Speers, Stefanie Hartman, Stephen Parsey, Steven Todd Smith, Tara Hannaford, Toni Parker, Victoria Dunn, Wendy Almasy, and Wendy Rogers.

Much gratitude to the team of people who helped me bring my visions to life: Alissa Bell, Candace Metzger, Gary Rosenberg, Mary Ellen Hettinger, Matt Starling, and Megan Wintory.

Preface

We all have struggles. Maybe not all the time, but on occasion, struggles creep into all of our lives. Having self-love helps support you during your struggles. When you love yourself, you don't judge yourself. When you stop judging yourself, you stop judging others. If we stopped judging ourselves, and therefore others, self-love becomes the cure for much of our society's issues.

This is harsh, but we need to be on the same page here (or else, no pages at all). First of all, you have to want to love yourself. If you don't want to love yourself, then please put this book down and get back to your stereotypical life of working 9 to 5 for someone else, likely doing work that is not aligned with your own dreams, living for weekends where you overuse substances to escape your own life, and attending social and family events out of guilt and obligation. These kinds of lifestyles do not allow the time to discover your true talents or dive deep into your heart's desires. This is what I like to call the "Go Fuck Yourself" lifestyle. You do you (on autopilot).

If you *do* want to love yourself, then you've got to dig deep and do the work. If you've decided you no longer want to live under someone else's made-up rules and you'd like to break free from the norms of society, awesome. Let's begin living the "Go Love Yourself" lifestyle. You do you (on a stick shift where you get to choose the gears). Cultivating self-love is the ultimate tool to have to live your best life. Go ahead and turn the page.

CHAPTER ONE

Selfie Does Not Equal Self-Love

"We've been so close for the last four years. We'd go to yoga, share meals, go shopping, go to movies, and buy each other thoughtful gifts. We both even moved into each other's houses during transition periods . . . we were essentially living the same kind of life. I'm not sure what else to say except I thought she was my best friend. She completely dropped off the map after our last brunch two months ago. I've recounted everything I said or did during the brunch and cannot find a moment that might have rubbed her the wrong way. I have no idea what happened." I took a moment to take a breath. "My best friend ghosted me!"

After I spoke my piece, I waited for my mentor, David, on the other end of the line to chime in with his two cents.

"Just because you seemingly lived the same lives on the outside doesn't mean you did on the inside. She couldn't keep up with you—not mentally, not emotionally, not spiritually. Her thoughts about herself are unkind. She lashes out at others when she doesn't get her way. She doesn't trust the process. What part of this matches who you are?"

I hadn't looked at it from that point of view (which is why everyone should have a mentor and/or a therapist). "You're right. None of this matches the person that I am—nor the person that I am becoming."

David went on. "This split was inevitable. I've seen the two of you in the same room. You open up your energy, warmly greeting people and giving them hugs. She closes her energy down, crossing her arms and not making eye contact with anyone. She couldn't even muster the courage to tell you the friendship was over!"

"I knew she was a little behind me in the self-development arena—and I never judged her for it—but wow, you're so right."

"You prioritize you. You take care of yourself. You know your worth. You don't allow anyone to mess with you, mentally, emotionally, or spiritually. You love yourself."

What does it mean to love oneself? This is a question I have repeated often over the last few years. We all have varied answers on what self-love is, as each of us has drastically different lives, tastes, and abilities. While self-love is going to look different for everyone, what all people who love themselves have in common is that they *made the choice* to do so.

I define self-love as making a series of personal strong choices. One must own everything about oneself—taking full responsibility for one's thoughts, choices, words, actions, moods, and previous ways of dealing with situations. Some of these past moments from your life may be embarrassing or shameful to admit and cop to, but someone who loves themselves takes full ownership of *all* of their choices. Self-love is a righteous knowing of oneself, one's identity. To get down to one's true identity, often we have to shed layers that don't serve us. We have to change, growing into a better version of ourselves. Self-love isn't just another form of self-development; it goes far deeper than that; it's soul development.

In theory, the journey of self-love is easy. It's the journey of getting to know oneself. In reality, the journey of getting to know oneself is downright challenging in this day and age when our social-media society constantly screams at us to be a certain way, like a certain thing, dislike a certain thing, be a certain size, wear a certain label, etc., which directly correlates with self-esteem issues. Selfie does not equal self-love.

> **Self-love is a righteous knowing of oneself, one's identity.**

What does loving oneself actually *mean* in our selfie society? The bottom line of self-love is that you've got to get to a point where you don't give a fuck about what others think about you or the choices that you make for yourself. (You have to get to a point where you're making choices for your higher good and not someone else's. *Ahem*, for example, family members—specifically parents—who project their desires onto you.)

I have traveled down a very personal path on my self-love journey. I have had massive leaps forward along with massive steps backwards. It's all been trial and error—but, such is life. I have reached a destination where I am compelled to share my journey thus far. There are so many learning curves on the journey of self-love. While some must be experienced as they happen, I have stories and advice to share with you with the intention of knocking some time off your journey so that you can get there faster and better equipped, sparing you some of the stumbles that I had along the way. I am the woman who's read every self-help book and actively applied the lessons to my life, and with that, I want to share with you the things that worked the best.

I have made drastic changes in my life over the last decade; some have been physical—such as moving from my hometown of Atlanta to Los Angeles when I was twenty-two. Friends and strangers alike always say how amazing it was that I moved to a large city where I didn't know anyone. I always looked at it as my heart's calling—I never experienced fear of being on my own; rather, I found it intoxicating, knowing I was pursuing my destiny. Another physical example is that I've lost sixty pounds in the last seven years—which I attribute to L.A.'s health and wellness culture. I often say that moving here saved my life—or at the very least, gave me an extra twenty years since I no longer consume fried everything.

While these are examples that anyone can physically see about me, the more important changes I have processed have been internal. When I was twenty-one, a friend of mine told me about vision boards. I have always been more apt to lean toward a glass half-full mentality, so I found the idea of visualizing the life you want with pictures and magazine clippings to be exciting. My first board included Monopoly money (to represent the finances it required to make the move and live on my own), veggies and fruit (to represent a healthier lifestyle), and a picture of the Hollywood sign (to represent my desire to live in L.A). Within six weeks, I was living in a house in the Hollywood Hills, about 1,000 feet away from the Hollywood sign. Coincidence? I don't think so.

I was sold on the whole idea of manifesting and keeping a positive mindset. In L.A., I began to meet like-minded people who were also into this kind of high vibe lifestyle and experiencing similar situations in their own lives. I always find it interesting when people make comments about how people in L.A. are plastic and fake. I know there are people out there in this category, yet I have had the exact opposite experience of Los Angeles. The more high vibe people I met and the more amazing stories I heard, the more I worked on my internal dialogue to switch from any hindering negative thoughts to upbeat positive thoughts.

I have been constantly evolving ever since, with no plan of stopping. I'm able to see my internal transformation in the form of my calmness, as in I no longer experience anxiety-filled thoughts. And, if they do pop up on occasion due to moments of being human, I'm able to quickly transform them and get back to a neutral state of being. I didn't realize this inner quality I worked so hard to achieve was visible to anyone else. But then I kept hearing a few things on repeat, including:

"What have you been doing?"

"How are you so happy and carefree all the time?"

"Bright energy is radiating out of you. How do you do it?"

The answer to all of these commonly heard questions boiled down to one answer: I had consciously made the strong choice to love myself. I am not better than you. I have simply created a life that allows me to make better decisions for myself—and if I did it, you can most certainly do it, too.

Clearly, I wasn't always like this. In my early-to-mid-twenties, I fully admit to being a mess. Even though I was continuously working on finding a positive mindset, that growth period came with a lot of confusing emotions, ego slamming and misunderstandings—between myself and also my loved ones. I was in the process of learning how to become a better version of myself; of course there were going to be hiccups along the way.

The thing about self-love is that no one really teaches us how exactly to do it. Throughout all my years of education, I don't recall ever sitting in a class being told the steps on how to cultivate self-love. Truly getting to know oneself is one of the most intimate journeys you will ever take, which undoubtedly includes vulnerability and honesty. Let me be the first to say that this is scary as these things are hard to confront—so much so, that most people shove it down, ignoring it, not living their best lives. Do you really want to be one of those people, not living your best life, missing out on your potential to shine your light out to the world? I certainly don't.

This book is the story of the strong choices I took to step into my self-loving lifestyle, detailing the patterns and practices I have that continually move me forward into living my best life. News flash—there will be *really* hard moments on the path, moments that will make you want to cry, quit, yell at the Universe—but guess what? Those moments are where the gold lies. Those moments are what I call the "Breakdowns to Breakthroughs."

This book and lifestyle is not for everyone. It's only for people who are ready to live up to their potential, make better choices, live their best lives, and achieve fulfillment and happiness in all areas and at all stages of their lives. Making the choice to cultivate self-love is a series of small changes you're going to have to make over time—and it will take time. There is no quick fix. You have to honor the process you're going through. This definitely means there will be uncomfortable moments, but please remember that being uncomfortable is the first step toward growth. So, embrace it!

You have to make changes in order to have a different life experience, and sometimes, those changes are hard to make. These steps on the road to change require an insane amount of courage. I believe in you and you must believe in yourself, too. When you start to learn who you truly are, a funny thing happens—you can no longer live in falsehood. You become your most authentic self.

CHAPTER TWO

Breakdown to Breakthrough

Breakdown—to cause to fall or collapse by breaking or shattering

Breakthrough—an act or instance of moving through or beyond an obstacle

No one really just wakes up one day and decides to love themselves. It's also rare for someone to be taught how to have self-love (unless you have a very self-aware parent, guardian or teacher in your youth). The choice is usually only made right after a significant moment. This is the moment I call the "Breakdown to Breakthrough." There are typically tears, yelling, screaming (probably mostly to the air, or God, or the Universe—whatever you like to call it), or sometimes it can be a very deep and serious, "I've had enough, I can no longer live like this" moment.

We often think of breakdowns as some psychological trauma that requires someone who cares about you dragging you to psychiatric care. What I am referring to is more about an internal shift. We need breakdowns to break through to the next level. Each part of your life requires a different version of yourself and sometimes you have to break down to break through—in other words, one step back followed by three giant leaps forward.

Some common examples of situations that might cause breakdowns are being in the wrong career, the wrong relationship, or essentially on the wrong path in general (if you're climbing the wrong ladder, while you may be going up, it's leading to nowhere). Breakdowns are bound to happen, especially when you keep trying to push, and the mountain you're pushing isn't moving—except for that giant avalanche about to fall down right smack on top of you.

I've had so many Breakdowns to Breakthroughs that they're nearly uncountable at this point. In fact, the one I had recently prompted me to write this book. They're one of the healthiest things I can do for myself. By allowing myself to break down (usually at home, alone—or with a very close friend who can handle and weather my emotions), I am able to feel and listen to what my intuition is dying to tell me.

My first memorable Breakdown to Breakthrough was when I was twenty-eight. It was New Year's Eve 2013 and I had just started my Saturn return. The Saturn return is what I like to call the astrological bar/bat mitzvah—when one truly becomes an adult (Mazel tov!). They happen to everyone, regardless if you believe in astrology or not, around ages twenty-seven to thirty. Saturn returns essentially shed away any last morsels of childhood behavior—the things that keep you from being a fully functioning adult. Often during the Saturn return, people will go through breakups or get married. They'll get a promotion or change career paths. They'll become parents or embark on a new, significant journey.

Whatever your Saturn return puts you through is always for your best interest, removing you from certain situations so that you can find yourself in better situations (though that can often be difficult to see while you're in the middle of your life crashing and exploding).

Your Saturn return will always jolt a piece of your life, particularly an inner piece (peace) of you, making you question your existence and path. This can be downright painful if you have no idea what's going on. Luckily, I knew about it and was prepared (as best as I could be) to handle the best of the worst of it.

I was in the beautiful kitchen of the house I shared with my at-that-time boyfriend. We'd been together for nearly four years and honestly, I was beginning to see that our relationship wasn't going to make it down the aisle, as we had originally thought. I had come to realize that I loved him, but I wasn't *in love* with him. I think he would say the same about me. Our friendship was strong, but ultimately, that didn't mean we were compatible in a life partnership.

He had taken a trip with his brothers to South America and I was home alone. I woke up early that morning (which would later become a predictor of when I'm about to have a Breakdown to Breakthrough) and went about my normal routine. I boiled the water for my yerba mate and checked my social media. A few minutes later, my daily alarm went off on my phone. The song I have set is "Halcyon and On and On" by Orbital. My dance teacher from my teen years (and now mentor), David, played this song every class during our company warm-up. Every time I hear it, it brings me back to those cherished moments and inspires me. Why not wake up every morning to something that inspires you?

My phone was on the other side of the room. I continued to pour my tea as the song played. As I stood there with the tea kettle in my hand, I had a massive realization of how depressing it was that my boyfriend wasn't with me on a holiday. Then it dawned on me that he didn't even ask me my thoughts and feelings about being without him on said holiday—he had planned the trip without considering me. It was New Year's Eve; we were supposed to kiss at midnight! I began to cry. Not so much about the fact that I was alone for the New Year, but rather about the fact that this person who was my partner had not even acknowledged me in this particular situation. This made me feel insignificant and unloved.

Then I started to cry harder, so much so that I dropped down to the ground and let it pour out of me. The Halcyon alarm was on repeat, playing over and over again. I told myself right then and there that I never wanted to be in another relationship where my thoughts and feelings were bypassed, and decisions were made without my consideration.

This moment was a big one for me as it helped push me forward into understanding my own self-worth. I had acknowledged that being treated like this was no longer acceptable. While this is certainly a Breakdown to Breakthrough, it's only a tremor compared to the next one I experienced eleven months later, when my Saturn return was in full swing.

Over the course of 2014, David and I both found ourselves in life-changing situations. I had broken up with my boyfriend, which prompted me to move out of the house we shared together. I knew myself well enough to acknowledge that moving into a one-bedroom completely alone post breakup was not going to go over well for me, especially after having lived in such a beautiful house. I knew I needed a drastic change—one with a bit of adventure.

I packed my belongings tightly into a storage unit while I exposed my heart wide open to explore what the future held for me. I called it my nomadic adventure. I house-sat, pet-sat, sublet, and stayed with friends. I was living in other people's houses, driving other people's cars, seemingly living other people's lives while fully embracing my own. In doing so, I got a sense of how others lived, which encouraged me to create more out of my own life. Most of my friends didn't grasp what the heck I was doing, as it was so unconventional, especially for my character. (I am a Cancer sun sign; home is where the heart is, after all.)

David, though, not only grasped it, he joined me. I got a call from him when I was about two months into my nine-month nomadic adventure. Coincidence that it was nine months? I essentially re-birthed myself, which is precisely what the Saturn return intends for you to do—whether you're conscious of it or not.

"I'm getting a divorce. I need to find a place to stay during my transition."

I chimed in, "Why don't you come stay with me?"

David arrived a few days later at what we now refer to as the Lakshmi House. Lakshmi is the Goddess of Abundance and Beauty in Hinduism and at this particular house I was subletting in Venice Beach, her presence was adamantly abundant. There were statues, blankets, magnets—basically, all gift shop items had been Lakshmized.

The night of Thanksgiving, David and I arrived back to our humble little Lakshmi abode. We had just come from a "Friendsgiving," where something I said had been misunderstood. Of course, my friends meant well, however, when I began to explain a personal situation to them, they immediately began to offer up suggestions that were premature, as I hadn't finished explaining the full story yet.

We stood in the Lakshmi kitchen (apparently, I like to have my Breakdowns to Breakthroughs in kitchens—which could also be another trait of being a Cancer sun sign), putting up the leftovers, when I looked at David and said, "I wasn't understood tonight. All of you skipped ahead of my story, not allowing me to finish."

David, with his wicked sense of humor mixed with humility, replied, "On behalf of all of us, but really just me at this point since I'm the only one here, we're sorry. Please tell me everything so I can better understand."

I began to mentally and emotionally spin, talking about everything that was on my mind. Thoughts about my ex and breakup, a new romantic interest that had recently appeared in my life, the issues I was having with my parents, my job, and everything else I could put into the blender. I started to cry. *Hard.* I was confused about everything. This breakdown was inevitable—and long overdue.

David stood there, taking it all in with me. "I think this is good. You've hit a point where you can't take it anymore. Cry it out. I'll go grab my rain boots."

And, so, what we now refer to as "the Lakshmi rainstorm" was born (my very own personalized Breakdown to Breakthrough nickname).

I stammered through my downpour of tears. "I know I'm in my Saturn return and I know it's supposed to be a radical transformation. But, I'm just not done yet. I have more to change. I feel like the turkey that people keep taking out of the oven to check the temperature, but I need more time. I'll ding when I'm ready. I want to live my best life possible, and this is my cave time to figure out how to create that for myself."

He chimed into my blended thoughts. "The good news is that you're completely aware of where you are, and you want to climb out from under-the-rock-bottom."

I thought back to an interview I'd seen not long before. "I'll think of it as the way J.K. Rowling referred to it—rock bottom allows you to build from a new, solid, steady foundation."

He said, "Isn't that what you're doing on this nomadic adventure of yours? Starting anew?"

"Bingo. Same with you, right?"

He said, "Yep. I have no other choice."

I nodded. "Same."

"All right. I'm in. Let's burn the ships."

I smirked, "I'll grab the lighter fluid."

Breakdowns to Breakthroughs are a gift. When you choose to burn the ships, the only option that remains is to rebuild. I am grateful for these opportunities. I'd much rather embrace the breakdowns rather than sludge through my life without being conscious of what's happening to (for) me.

Now that we've gone over examples of what a Breakdown to Breakthrough can look like, let's talk about what happens after. You're going to have to get really honest with yourself. Like *really* uncomfortably honest. The kind of honesty that requires vulnerability; the kind of honesty that requires acknowledging your faults. This is undoubtedly the hardest part of the journey and there is no bypassing it. Tackle what's on your mind—it's likely the precise thing that led to your breakdown. You either get honest and move forward with your newfound truth or you stay the same (likely repeating the same situations over and over again—wash, rinse, repeat). Getting honest with yourself is a vital step to changing, as it allows you to see what exactly needs to be changed. All change starts from within; it starts with the courageous choice to make the change.

After you have a breakdown, another part of the breakthrough is discovering your identity. I find that most people go through their lives not truly knowing who they are; rather, they're just doing things out of habit or because their friends, family, and/or boss told them to. In case no one has ever told you this before, you get to design your own life. How exciting is it to not only consciously discover who you really are, but to then live out your life as you want to?! It's a full-on adventure!

> **All change starts from within; it starts with the courageous choice to make the change.**

Once you've gotten honest with yourself, own your story and experiences, and acknowledge what you need to change, you have to start implementing. With one step at a time, you'll begin to learn about yourself—what you like and don't like, what you will and won't tolerate, what makes you feel aligned and unaligned—all of the things that make you, well, *you.* Self-love is the ultimate knowing of your identity. Know what you want and do what it takes to get it. The only way out is (break) through.

CHAPTER THREE

Sacredness

We have a real crisis—people don't know how to love themselves because people don't understand their own sacredness. People are suffering because they don't know that they are sacred. Universal fact: if you're a conscious being living on this planet right now, you are sacred (so start acting like it!).

The word *sacred* has many interpretations. It can relate to religious texts, a person, place, or thing that is blessed or holy—it is essentially something that has an infinite amount of respect. But what does it mean to *embody* being sacred?

If you've stepped foot into a yoga studio, you've undoubtedly heard lines like, "You are a soul having a human experience." While I certainly do believe this, let's break this down into a more practical manner, discussing the relationship we have with our mind, body, and spirit, and how all three must be integrated into every arena of our lives to be living a life fully embodying our own sacredness.

We're all walking around aware that we have a mind and a body because we can actively sense that we do (plus, science can clearly prove it). However, how does one acknowledge that we also have a spirit? For me, I grew up seeing auras and energy around people. I didn't realize that this was one of my gifts—I thought everyone saw what I saw, just as you assume that everyone sees the sky as blue. When I moved to Los Angeles in my early twenties, I began to meet other people with similar gifts, which not only helped me understand myself more, but expanded my views on life and spirituality. My path to understanding my connection to the divine—*my* sacredness—began to unfold.

The more I dug further into my own spirituality—meaning many long and deep talks with like-minded people, readings with mediums and astrologers, practicing meditation and yoga, crystal healings and reiki sessions, reading all sorts of metaphysical books and attending seminars on how to live your best life—the easier my life became. I began to understand my purpose. Psychic energy has never scared me, as I'm someone who wants to know as much as I possibly can about everything, from every angle, so that I can best assess my life and the situations I find myself in. Plus, with my third eye being wide open having seen auras my entire life, it's hard to deny that this spiritual—and sacred—energy exists. I don't believe that working with psychic energy alters the timeline or the destiny of your life. Instead, you have free will and the choices that you make day in and day out alter and shape your life. I have always found that participating in the metaphysical world allows me to make better choices in my life since I have been provided with a grander view on things—like a helicopter pilot who can see the traffic from up above.

With that being said, one of my best guy friends is an atheist—science is everything to him. (That smartphone you've got? His dad helped create, so, of course, science is his life). Since my kind of spirit talk isn't scientifically proven like the mind and body are, he's just not on board with my "hippie-dippy" ways. My own personal belief is that we (as humans) have to learn how to combine science and spirit together to truly understand our Universe (and ourselves).

He and I have shared many discussions on our beliefs and while he doesn't see or believe what I believe, he always acknowledges that I am happier and have my life more balanced than most—and also that I'm always able to see the positive in everything. He has asked me a few times before how I'm able to live my life with such a positive outlook. I have many "spiritually loaded" answers to this question including that I think you must believe in something—the Universe, God, whatever—to ultimately believe in yourself, as when you have faith in a higher power, it's far easier to have faith in yourself and understand that you have a purpose for being alive. However, the most logical—and true—response to his question is that I *choose* to see the positive because I want to live my best life, which is part of my self-love. What you decide to focus your mind on is a choice. I don't bypass the negative things—I have certainly analyzed why things have happened in my life, both good and bad. However, I choose to see the positive because I know having a positive outlook makes for a better life experience.

I embody my sacredness, as a human being living in the twenty-first century, by respecting myself (and others, acknowledging that everyone is sacred). You are sacred. You have a sacred mind, a sacred body, and a sacred spirit. Embody your sacredness by respecting all three. If the word *sacred* means "regarded with great respect and reverence by a particular thing," according to the dictionary, make that thing *you*.

MIND

To respect your mind, you must first acknowledge that your thoughts create things. To be ultimately respectful to your mind and your sacredness, you must transform your negative thoughts into positive ones, only thinking about the things you *do* want, not the things you *don't* want.

We are made of energy and energy's natural state is to create. The creation of your experience starts in your mind. You are exactly what you think. Your mind—and mindset— holds your perception of the world. If you want to change something about your life, the first step is to change your mindset about it.

I began to understand just how powerful this concept of thought creation was when my first vision board with the Hollywood sign on it landed me within walking distance of the iconic sign. Sixteen months after my move, I created another vision board. But this time, it was for my entire life, not just for what I wanted to achieve in the near future. I included photos that represented the career I wanted to have, things like yoga and meditation to expand my spirituality, and images of what it would feel and be like when meeting my future husband and eventually create our family together. I still have this vision board and look at it daily. When something on it comes to fruition, I put a small little check on it, acknowledging my gratitude for creating it into my life. One piece of advice: be careful what you glue down—you just might get it!

During the first year and a half living of living in Los Angeles, I was extremely blessed to have my parents' financial support while I attended school and learned to navigate freelance life. Then the economy shifted. Both of my parents have spent their lives in the housing, mortgage, and real estate industry. While, thankfully, they survived the economy crash more so than many others did, they could no longer fully financially support me. To be fair, I was twenty-four-years-old; it was time for me to support myself.

My parents told me they could only cover my rent for two more months and then it would be on me. I began to "throw mud," as my dad describes it. "Throwing mud" at the wall is a southern metaphor to describe applying for jobs. When you throw mud, eventually something will stick.

I spent those two months relentlessly sending out my resume to job applications, hundreds of e-mails to people I knew and people I didn't, and taking random day gigs that brought in a little bit of cash. I spent a few hours every day actively doing the work on my end—stirring the energy—to get money coming in. The worst-case scenario was that I could have moved back to Georgia to my parents' house. It's not like I ever thought I would have been without a roof over my head and food in my tummy.

However, I knew my purpose was to be in L.A. I didn't know why—or what exactly my purpose was at that point—but I knew this was exactly where I was supposed to be. I had faith and belief that the Universe was going to provide me with the means to stay here. My journey to explore and discover my purpose and passions outweighed my fear toward it. I knew something would stick, as that's the way throwing mud works, even if it takes time and pulls through at the very last second, a type of Hail Mary if you will. The Universe *always* provides—even more so to those who believe so.

Simultaneously while throwing mud, I began to recite affirmations daily. An affirmation is a declaration used to help shift your thoughts to a more positive state. The types of affirmations I use always start with "I am." "I can." Or "I will." Then I fill in the rest of the sentence with whatever I'm trying to accomplish. When I started to use affirmations to shift from a lack-of-abundance mentality to a full-of-abundance mentality, I always recited them in the shower, as I've always felt a connection to water (another Cancer sun sign aspect). My intention was that as I washed away the dirt from my body, creating a clean physical space, I also could wash away negative thoughts, creating a positive mental space. One of the affirmations I said on constant repeat during that time period was, "I am financially self-sufficient." Any time I would have a moment of self-doubt or discouragement on the job front (not to mention, looking at my dwindling bank account), I would recite this affirmation until I was blue in the face. I basically tricked myself into believing that I had money—even though I could barely afford groceries. This is one of the major keys to manifesting—fake it till you make it.

I had eight dollars left in my bank account and a nearly maxed-out credit card when I got a call from a producer I had worked with the year before. He asked me to meet him at Kings Road Café later that day to discuss his upcoming project. I got in my Explorer (a total metaphor for the kind of life I lived during my early twenties) and headed to West Hollywood. I ordered a latte that was six dollars and tipped one dollar. With that one dollar remaining in my bank account, I was offered a job on the crew of his film, which covered my rent and expenses for the next four months.

Not long after, when I was a bit more stable in my finances and the paychecks were coming in from the job (the reciting of the affirmations never stopped), I vowed to myself out loud that I would continue to do the hard work—change any negative thoughts I had into positive ones. The kind of life I wanted to live required, if not demanded, this kind of work. I also told myself that I would never have such low funds in my bank account ever again. Those days were behind me and I had learned my first of many lessons on how to manifest abundance.

When a moment of fear hits, I acknowledge that it's just a passing moment. I quickly change my outlook to a positive one, reversing the negative to a positive. If fake it till you make it is a key to manifesting, then believing in yourself, your passion and your purpose—your sacredness—are keys to overcoming fear.

When you want to achieve something, you have to exercise two factors—your thoughts about it and your actions toward it. You can be doing as many affirmations (or actions) as breaths you take, but if you're not doing the actions (or affirmations and thoughts) to bring your goals to fruition, it's pretty meaningless, as both have to align to properly manifest. Treat your thoughts with utmost respect. When you're able to conquer your mind, unconvolute your thoughts, and match them with your actions, this is the ultimate respect to your sacredness.

BODY

There are multiple ways to respect your body, such as feeding yourself nutritious foods and exercising often. While I will cover the physicality in more expansive detail in a future chapter, what I want to focus on right now is sacred sexuality.

In my early twenties, I had casual sex with men who were not my boyfriends, hoping that by sleeping with them it would potentially create a relationship. I was so wrong—and so insecure. I was also overweight. It didn't feel great to be in my body. I often questioned if I was pretty enough for a man to be attracted to me. A man who gave me attention could easily get me in bed, as I was starving for affection. I was taking what I thought was "love" from any man who wanted to sleep with me, clueless that I should be giving love to *myself* first and foremost. When I look back to this time period in my life, I remember a lot of confusion and sadness on my part. Sex was always disappointing. I wanted to express emotion and love while in bed, which was never going to happen with hookups or in friends-with-benefits situations.

When I lost my first 30 pounds, my self-esteem increased, and I did eventually meet a nice boyfriend—the same boyfriend I spent four years with. We didn't sleep with one another until after we had already established that we were in a relationship (which came after establishing a solid friendship). Finally, for the first time in my life, I was able to experience the kind of physical-meets-emotional connection I was craving.

After our breakup, many of my friends encouraged me to get back out there and date, to find someone to have rebound sex with. I had been in a loving, caring, committed relationship for four years where we respected one another (and snuggled and made pancakes together post-coitus). Rebound sex—or sex in general with someone I wasn't in love with—didn't sound appealing. However, after a few months, I did find myself out on some dates. And I did sleep with one of them. I got caught up in the moment of enjoying being desired. But afterward, I felt completely empty and drained. I wasn't in love with this man, I didn't want to snuggle with him and I certainly didn't want to make pancakes with him. So why had I just let this man inside of my body? I made a new rule right then and there regarding my own sacred sexuality. I would not sleep with anyone until I was in a committed relationship again—with someone special, someone I loved, someone who loved me, someone who understood that sex is sacred, and someone who got excited that snuggling and pancakes were part of the deal. I didn't just want a man, I wanted *the* man.

I've heard so many women say, "I can't sleep with him on the first few dates because I don't want him to think I'm a slut." I didn't want to be of this mentality so I simply removed myself completely from the equation by choosing my sacred sexuality over casual sexuality. I began to think of the kind of woman my future husband would respect and then I became that woman. I was willing to do the work on myself to get the kind of man I desired—and this was part of the work. So, off I went on my newfound life of celibacy.

A few months went by, and then a year went by, followed by another year, then another. I realized that being completely alone, observing myself and really getting to understand who I was sans any kind of man or relationship in the picture, was one of the best choices I have ever made for myself. (Side note: I did invest in a high-quality vibrator because something's gotta give. Plus, masturbation is a literal definition of self-love.)

I realized that once I made this choice, all of the creepy guys who had tried to make awkward and inappropriate moves on me disappeared. I was no longer attracting people who treated me poorly because I was no longer treating myself poorly. A guy friend of mine told me that the way I carried myself represented "wife quality" and that only men who were serious about moving forward in their own lives would show interest in me at this point. He was so right. Nowadays, respectable and virile men are the ones who talk to me—men who respect themselves and want a woman who does the same. Like attracts like.

Having the gift of seeing auras, I also inherently understood that when you are physically intimate with someone, your auras merge together, making sex a very sacred act (sex: Sacred Energy eXchange). This is a totally wonderful experience for people who are in love, as it brings you closer, bonding your energies together. However, if you're having meaningless and emotionless sex, it can leave a ton of debris and clutter in your aura, which can then go on to affect your energy, thoughts, and overall life circumstances. If the rando you just slept with has issues with self-doubt, depression, guilt, shame, etc., guess what just got left on your aura? All of their shit.

When you're in a relationship with someone, you're usually aware of your partner's issues (and they yours) and have acceptance of them. In loving relationships, there's a give and receive, where you both help each other transmute through issues with love. However, the randos can often leave behind some heavy debris that you're not even aware of. I can see it floating around on so many people in our Tinder culture. It's extremely upsetting, as most have no clue they're swirling in an energetical mess, being so disconnected from their own sacredness.

I truly believe energy merging is what all the religious texts are referring to when they essentially say, "Save it for marriage." And, while I don't believe that that's practical for most in this day and age, I certainly agree that you should only be sleeping with someone who loves you and you also love them. Cherish yourself and attract someone who also cherishes themselves, then cherish each other together. That's sacred sexuality at its best. (Side note: my choice of celibacy until a committed relationship might be an extreme choice in some people's opinion. You don't have to be as extreme as me. My point is to know your choice and how all of it affects you.)

If you're on any type of self-discovery journey, one of the healthiest things you can do for yourself is remain single while trying to figure yourself out. Learn to stand on your own two feet, get to know yourself fully. Until you're very clear about who you are and what you want out of life, it's not appropriate—or fair—to bring in a partner. Plus, working on yourself—making yourself healthy in mind, body, and spirit—means you'll attract someone on a similar path, who also wants to create a healthy relationship together. You have to feel very secure in your own self-love to have a successful relationship—not only with a partner but more importantly with yourself.

If you are with a partner and decide to go on a self-love journey, one of two things will likely happen. Your partner will join you and go on his or her own version of a self-love journey. Or, you'll do so much work on yourself that you might outgrow your partner. I've seen it happen so many times and it's nothing to fear. Know that you are always exactly where you're supposed to be and with whom you're supposed to be with.

For me, being alone for many years helped me raise my standards. I learned how to respect myself, my body, and my sacred sexuality. What my celibacy path taught me is that I don't *need* a partner. Rather, I *want* a partner. I have learned to have a very fulfilling relationship with myself, learning to take care of myself and all of my needs, creating my own happiness. When I do merge together in a relationship again, I will rely on myself to make me happy—as that's not my partner's responsibility (his responsibly is to make himself happy). We will simply add more joy and happiness to each other's lives because we love ourselves—and one another. I understand that my body is sacred and deserves to be shared only with someone who acknowledges that. This is my sacred sexuality.

SPIRIT

I was speaking with a friend of mine not too long ago when he asked me how I knew the information I had just shared.

I said, "I just know."

"This isn't something you could just know."

I said with conviction, "It's a gut feeling."

"You can't trust your gut. Guts are often wrong."

I acknowledge that his experiences have led him to this belief. Yet, I know that my gut, instinct, and intuition are never wrong. I've developed an intimate relationship with these aspects of my spirit and they never lead me astray.

Two months later, I was out shopping when I came

across a beautiful piece of art. I knew immediately when I saw it that it was for my friend—the one who doesn't trust his gut. This piece of art displayed his first love: music. I purchased it and brought it to him a few days later.

He said, "This couldn't have come at a more perfect time. How did you know?"

"Gut feeling."

He went on to tell me some of his recent personal experiences. While I previously didn't know the details of his difficulties, my intuition knew that this piece of art was for him. As it turns out, it was specifically to inspire him and help him remember his true nature. You don't always need to know why or how; your intuition will always lead you down the right path.

Many say that women are far more in tune with their intuition and that men can easily rely on their instinct. I believe these are essentially the same sacred guiding lights. Perhaps different vehicles, yet they lead you to the same destination. Your intuition, inner voice, instinct, Higher Self, gut, and heart—or whatever you want to call it—are all the same in regard to spirit. They are all there for you to understand your sacredness.

An important aspect of acknowledging your sacredness is developing trust in yourself—and the Universe. Listen and understand what spirit is trying to communicate with you. To do this, let's talk about the stuff we're made of. The first step of opening up to hearing your intuition is to understand you are energy. Energy is a vibration, always traveling between different frequencies. When you feel good about life (mind, body, and spirit), I call this being in your *high vibe*. What it means is that your soul energy has aligned with a higher vibration frequency that is for your best path. When you feel kind of *"meh"* about life, I call this being in your *low vibe*. We all experience highs and lows in life, and it's totally okay to embrace when you are in your low vibe so that you can figure out how to get back to your high vibe. I will discuss this in more detail further along in another chapter.

Many of us have had the experience of a few seconds before a song plays on the radio, where we know which particular song will be coming on next. Then when it plays, we get excited, "I knew that would be the next song!" This is a perfect example to explain how we are made up of energy, going through our daily experiences tapped into differently tuned frequencies.

I learned to further develop my relationship with my energy—my intuition—by opening up my mind to the signs and synchronicities that happen all the time. What some call coincidences, I began to call my *sacred spirit*. When synchronicities happen, I never think it's just a coincidence. I take it as a sign from the Universe, showing me that I'm on the right path. Often these indicators are very humorous. I find that the spirit world is filled with lots of laughter—spirit doesn't take things as seriously as we humans do.

Another friend of mine (who is so incredibly cerebral and not even open to the conversation of what the Universe may or may not be) told me that he didn't believe that things happened in some sort of divine order; rather everything that was happening was just a coincidence. I met a woman at a business function (3,000 miles away from my home), where we started talking about relationships and she told me about her former boyfriend. Come to find out, it was my friend's brother. I had also purchased a simple ring about a year before this friend and I met. This ring became one of my frequently worn pieces. A few years later, someone asked me where I had purchased it. I pulled up the e-mail from Etsy and I noticed the name of the ring was the full name—first and last—of my friend. My mouth dropped wide open. I took a screenshot of the e-mail, texted it to him, then called to explain. His response? "Coincidence."

I certainly view these kinds of things as synchronicities, messages from Spirit encouraging me that all is on track in my world. I honor and respect these magic moments and signs from the Universe as I acknowledge that I'm aligned with my Higher Self, my spirit. Do you find "coincidences" happen frequently? Are you paying attention to them? Don't discredit them. They're a message for you, from your intuition.

I often see that if someone is not listening to their intuition, ignoring the signs and synchronicities, that life can have a lot of unnecessary chaos and frustration. That's how energy works. When you are aligned with your spirit, things flow much easier. When you're disconnected from your spirit, things don't go so easily.

If you're having a hard time seeing or finding the signs in your life, simply ask to see them. Say a prayer or set an intention to be aware of all

Positive thoughts equal a higher vibration.

the things going on around you that are meant for you to take notice, to learn from. Pray with your eyes wide open as the signs are often right in front of you.

Your vibration is a direct reflection of what you are experiencing. Your thoughts control your vibrations. It's actually a really simple formula. Positive thoughts equal a higher vibration. Negative thoughts equal a lower vibration. Use your mind, carefully crafting your thoughts to tap in to your spirit—your sacredness. I believe this is the secret to creating the life of your dreams. We are all made of energy and once you learn about your own energy by conquering your own thoughts, you can live any kind of way you wish to, literally seeing your dreams come to fruition.

Follow the signs. Follow your heart. Follow your intuition. Listen to that inner spark; it's trying to tell you something important. Following your intuition is the following of your path; it will always lead you to where you need to be. Trust that eventually all of the dots will inevitably connect. This is the ultimate honoring of your sacredness.

I believe that to fully understand who you are and what you're here to accomplish in life, you have to consciously integrate all three aspects of mind, body, and spirit. If the root of everything is self-love, the seed is sacredness. Sacred self-love is your essence. This is your core. A infinite amount of respect is due to you as you are sacred.

CHAPTER FOUR

Strong Choices

How you do one thing is how you do everything. Let's repeat that because this is important. *How you do one thing is how you do everything.* Everything you do in your life is a choice. Understanding this empowers you. When you are in charge of your choices, you are empowered. When you are empowered, you love yourself.

Exploring my own identity gave my life meaning. Not that I had come from a place with no meaning, but rather I was on society's hamster wheel: graduate high school, attend a four-year university, marry before twenty-five, have some babies in the next few years, raise those babies, retire, travel, have grandbabies—you get the point. One of the best choices I ever made was to get off the hamster wheel

> How you do one thing is how you do everything.

when I moved to Los Angeles, leaving behind all that the hamster wheel could provide me (which was for me, a very predictable life).

My intuition knew that I was born for something other than predictability; something that I would have to create from scratch, by myself. Something that would require me to dig deep into my own spiritual being so that I could understand myself and my purpose.

I define making a strong choice as making a wholehearted, committed decision. A decision that steers your life in the direction of your dreams and goals. I made the choice—or rather choices, over and over again—to find a better way to live my life. Each phase of life requires a different version of ourselves. I find myself constantly evolving, making different choices as different circumstances arise.

The first strong choice I made was to understand my sacredness, making it a priority. I knew that once I understood myself more in depth, I would understand my entire life and path on a deeper level. I was yearning to know myself—so that I could learn to trust myself and also learn to trust the path that my intuition was leading me down. I wanted to get to know myself so well, well enough to never doubt my feelings or the thoughts I had, trusting my intuition fully. Once I began to rely on my intuition, magical things started happening.

Earlier I said that self-love is the ultimate knowing of your identity. So, what does getting to know oneself look like? For me, my yoga mat became the mirror of what I needed to learn about myself.

NAMASTE

Namaste—Sanskrit, "the light in me honors the light in you" (pronounced na-ma-stay)

After I told myself (and the Universe) that I would never have so little in my bank account ever again, and after my production job ended, I decided to take a part-time assistant job for a celebrity yoga teacher. Not only did this job provide me with a steady income and flexible hours so I could still do production work, but it also opened up a whole other spiritual world to me: the one on the Westside of Los Angeles, where the scene was all about meditation, the music of Krishna Das, green juices, and tofu tacos.

Ironically, during my two and a half years of working in the yoga world, I rarely did any physical yoga. I would go to a class on occasion, but most days I was so sick of typing out Sanskrit documents, the last thing I wanted to do was go to an hour and a half class and listen to Sanskrit. Once I left that job, I took a solid year off from the yoga scene, not entering a single studio or doing a single down dog.

Eventually, I realized that I wasn't doing so well. My job and relationship were taking every ounce of everything I had out of me. At lunch one day, as I was explaining how drained I was, my friend Glenda (as in the Good Witch) said to me, "Let me know when you want to come back to yoga."

Glenda would casually mention it every few weeks, in e-mails or during random conversations on the phone.

I would say, "Yeah, yeah . . . I know." with no real intention of making it to class anytime soon.

A few months went by. With my hectic work, travel schedule, and inevitable breakup, I was at wit's end with *everything*. It was also during my Saturn return, so I knew I had to make the best of the worst of it. I realized that I could no longer go on in this stress; I needed to take care of myself—like I had been taking care of others (my job, my ex, my friends). I picked up the phone and called Glenda. "What time is class today?"

"Four-fifteen PM."

"Okay, I'll meet you there."

That is where it all *re*-started. It officially started when I had the yoga job but as I have come to learn, sometimes it is the restart that matters the most. I walked out of that first class feeling amazing. I was sweaty, worked out, and centered. Plus, I hadn't been on my phone for an hour and a half. I didn't even realize how desperately I needed a break from all the dinging notifications that ran my life.

Feeling so high from yoga was something I wanted more of in my life. So, I made a choice. I signed up for a membership and began going to that 4:15 PM class, with Glenda by my side, cheering me on, three times a week for a solid year. Trust me when I say there were days when I didn't want to go. I would have rather stayed home, eating potato chips and watching Netflix, especially if I was hormonal or feeling mentally, physically, and/or emotionally run down. But those were the days I needed the yoga the most. Going into a class not feeling my best allowed me to face those feelings and emotions head on, on my mat. Sometimes those emotions were best dealt with in Child's Pose (a resting pose), and other times they were best dealt with in a vigorous *Surya B* flow. Each day was a different experience on my mat yet the *Savasana* (Corpse Pose, where you rest at the end of each class) remained consistent, zenful.

Consciously deciding to make my yoga practice a part of my life was the beginning of me laying a new foundation. The practice allowed me space. I would take three hours out of my day to attend this specific class—the class itself was an hour and a half and the commute to and from was often another hour and a half. (I was coming from Beverly Hills to

Santa Monica and back again at the hours of 3:30 PM and 6:30 PM. **#traffuck**.)

A few months into my commitment to the practice, I had more energy, my body was in better shape, and I was accomplishing more tasks than ever before—which was kind of strange to think about, given the three hours it took out of my day. What in the world *was* I doing with those three hours *before* yoga, with nothing to show for it? Yoga helped shape my body and brain; clearing the clutter from my thoughts so that I could create a more productive and flourishing way of living. Life just simply got better in all arenas while practicing yoga—with my thoughts becoming more focused and my inner wisdom being more clearly heard and understood.

I am a natural giver (with that Cancer sun sign of mine, I yearn to nurture everyone), but with that being said, I need a way to fill back up on everything I am giving out. The more yoga I did, the more service I could give to my job, family, and friends. Yoga is the true example of taking care of yourself so you're able to take care of the world around you.

Another interesting thing I began to notice was that for the first time ever, I could feel my body—which is an interesting statement coming from someone who grew up dancing. However, up until around this time, I'd had pharmaceuticals in my bloodstream—a cocktail of antidepressants from age seventeen to twenty-one to help regulate my migraines, and also the birth control pill—for nearly a decade. I was disconnected to my own being—mind, body, spirit—in all situations, I was comfortably numb. By the time I started my yoga practice, I was no longer taking any sort of pill. My yoga practice helped me become uncomfortably un-numb.

Sometimes, life is uncomfortable, especially during Saturn returns, yet without the discomfort, how would we ever know what we needed to change and work on? Have no fear, it's just a transition; this too shall pass.

Along with feeling my body for the first time in ages, I connected more with my spirit. Yoga poses are ancient wisdom, designed to align you with higher energy. You can't commit to vigorous vinyasa flow yoga classes three times a week and not feel the difference in your mind, body, and spirit. I was tuning into my own intuition, my own sacredness, more so than ever. I would get to *Savasana* not only feeling zenful but would often have mini epiphanies of whatever I was searching for on that specific day. Yoga cleared my head so that I could hear my spirit communicating with me via my intuition.

They say your yoga mat is your mirror. My yoga practice certainly held up a mirror to my own reflection, showing me what I needed to learn. I have asked hundreds of people why they do yoga—and what I hear from almost everyone is, "It changed my life." Yoga changed my life (and continues to change my life) because it helped me get to know myself.

FORESHADOWING

In my early twenties, I had a mentor who was very intuitive. One of the first high vibe people I met in Los Angeles, he had a keen ability to see things about people, specifically their purpose. He told me that the self-growth lessons I learn on my personal path must be taught to others to help them live up to their potential. In other words, what I learn, I must teach. I remember him saying, "As your life unfolds, so will your work."

He also told me that once I was able to master emotional intelligence and self-love, that I would be able to live the life of my dreams. Of course, at that time, I didn't fully understand what that meant. He also told me I was a writer. I tilted my head with confusion as writing wasn't really a part of my life, other than some random journaling.

Around age twenty-nine, I made the choice to start writing my stories, including the journey of finding my self-worth in regard to relationships, analyzing—while not judging—all of the previous choices I had made. I had been trying to have relationships with others without fully knowing myself, giving out love to everyone but myself. The writing was cathartic and very eye opening. I was able to understand myself more than ever by fully taking responsibility for all of my past choices, all while being extremely vulnerable and honest with myself. The truth is, you have to go through vulnerability before empowerment. Vulnerability is required in the journey of getting to know yourself.

Writing got me high—similar to yoga—and I was (and still am) addicted to the high vibe. Then I remembered what my mentor had told many moons ago—I was writing my stories to share with the world. The more I began to love myself, the more I realized it was my purpose to share my stories with others to help them come into their own version of self-love.

EMOTIONAL INTELLIGENCE

Have you ever yelled at your significant other/parent/close friend, with them yelling back, and then from there it escalated to a full-fledged fight that you can barely even remember what you were fighting about once it's all said and done? I have—many times in my youth, and it continued up until the breakup with my former boyfriend. I had zero emotional intelligence. I was letting my emotions run the entire show, which was often a messy (and exhausting) outburst.

Part of my transformation into self-love was about understanding my emotions. And, getting a grip on them. I vowed to myself to work on controlling those outbursts. I realized that no self-respecting future husband of mine was going to deal with my childish ways (nor I to his). No one wants an emotionally unstable person around; those types of people create chaos. Nowadays, if anyone starts to get heated in their emotions toward me, I walk away from the situation, regardless of how much I love said person. I tell them to talk to me when they've calmed down. I respect myself too much to let someone else's lack of emotional intelligence interfere with my vibe. I choose peace.

How does one become emotionally intelligent, releasing the past patterns of messy outbursts? Does it develop over time with a life of lessons and certain situations that teach us? Certainly. But is there a way to tap into it faster? Certainly. We've already touched on how the thoughts you have are a direct correlation of your experience. We've gone over how thoughts bring forth manifestation (of things desired and also things not desired), but thoughts also play a contributing part to our emotions.

So, what is emotional intelligence? Emotions are feelings that come and go, yet they are there for a reason—to listen to, to understand, and most importantly; to feel. However, you shouldn't let your feelings overtake you and run the show. This is where the intelligence comes into play.

Thoughts trigger emotions. Be conscious of your thoughts to understand your emotions. Transforming your thoughts to healthy, positive ones requires self-awareness. Your thoughts are vibrations that imprint onto your life experience—from things that happen outside of you (the world in general) to the things that happen inside of you (emotions). When you have positive, uplifting thoughts, your outer and inner worlds begin to reflect that. Uplifting thoughts equal uplifting life.

First Step

There are three steps I used to develop emotional intelligence. The first step is to acknowledge your feelings, your emotions. This one is probably easier for women than it is for men, as women are taught that it's acceptable to cry and feel, whereas men are taught the exact opposite—to suck it up and carry on. Man, oh man, that "suck it up and carry on" mentality has really created a huge disharmony in our society. I won't carry on too much on this subject, but I do think if men were taught from an early age that it's okay to be expressive and properly feel their emotions, there would be less violence and more balance in the world.

If you can't feel your way through your emotions, then you don't know yourself. Let's repeat that. If you can't feel your way through your emotions, then you don't know yourself. Your feelings

> **If you can't feel your way through your emotions, then you don't know yourself.**

often relate to your intuition—in other words, your feelings are trying to tell you something. Emotional intelligence means coming into alignment with your intuition. So how does one really feel feelings? Most importantly, by letting them be with you instead of shoving them aside or yelling during an outburst. Give yourself the gift of really feeling your feelings, using them as a guidance system to understanding yourself.

Second Step

The second step is to process said feelings, whether good or bad. But we'll mostly focus on the more difficult feelings at the moment, given those are the harder ones to process. Once you have a firm grasp on, "What's going on with me? Oh! These are feelings that are arising! I'm going to consciously acknowledge them!" then you can begin to process them. While studying my own emotional intelligence, I started to implement different techniques to understand the flow of my emotions better. The thing that worked best for me was that I made the choice to stay still. Meaning I practiced not reacting until I had a firmer grasp on the entire picture. This took away my past pattern of outbursts. Sometimes a Breakdown to Breakthrough will happen during my stillness, which always reveals to me more information I need to better understand whatever I'm processing. This practice completely changed my life. Staying still is where I found the ability to trust that the answer will always come to me in due time.

Third Step

The third step is to make choices only after you have under-stood and processed your feelings. When you make choices prior to processing, you're making choices on unstable ground, in the heat of the moment. This ultimately makes the choice a weak one (not to mention, chaotic), given you are lacking a strong foundation. By making choices after you've processed your feelings, you are taking control of your situation, your vibration, from a strong and sturdy place. Choosing to respond to situations from a strong foundation instead of reacting from a weak foundation is a lovely lesson for all aspects of life. When you stand strong from having processed your emotions, you can't be knocked down.

Choosing to process your emotions is how you take control of your life. These strong choices are what empower you. When you can create emotional intelligence where you are in control of your thoughts, processing your feelings, and making strong choices, this is living an empowered life, a life filled with self-love.

TAKING RESPONSIBILITY

The second strong choice I made after putting my sacredness first was to take responsibility for all of my *previous* thoughts and actions. Loving yourself means making the choice to take massive responsibility for everything in your life: your current situation, your past situations, and your future situations. Because we are made of energy, we are always creating everything around us—consciously and subconsciously. Yes—everything in your life you have created one way or another which is why it's so incredibly important to be aware of your thoughts, your vibrations, and the words that you speak to yourself and to others. Self-love without self-awareness isn't a thing.

Taking responsibility is often a difficult practice that many people avoid, pushing it under the metaphorical "rug," creating even more issues to deal with in the future. Whatever is under the rug always comes out eventually. Do yourself a favor and toss the rug out, so it's not even an option.

I had to take responsibility for my health and that was a very hard thing for me to cop to. It was my own fault due to the choices I had made that I ended up weighing 205 pounds at age twenty-three. For a long time, I attributed my weight gain on the Freshman 15 (followed by the Sophomore 15, Junior 15, and Senior 15), the culture of the South (fried everything), and that my parents fed me fast food my entire childhood and had genetically modified foods in the cabinets and fridge instead of organic foods.

By the time I was eighteen and out of my parents' house, I continued to eat whatever I wanted, when I wanted, knowing it wasn't good for me. I was seeing the weight pile on—yet I refused to change my habits. I was stubborn, and I didn't want anyone's advice on the subject. I ate fast food at 2 AM. I consumed 3,000-plus calories a day and didn't exercise. These are facts about my health and wellness journey, but until I started to actually pay attention to my health, I used these as excuses—shoving them all under my metaphorical rug. Now looking back, I can cop to the fact that these were my own choices, choices that inevitably led to me weighing 205 pounds.

Once I was able to take responsibility for the choices I made, I was able to make better choices moving forward. This lead me on a health and wellness journey, expanding over the course of multiple years, where I lost 60 pounds and switched to an organic diet. Without having copped to my previous choices, I doubt I would be able to be as grateful as I am now having come out on the other side.

The same goes for past relationships. In my early twenties, I dated men who didn't treat me well. I had to cop to the fact that I didn't treat myself well, so I was attracting men to treat me exactly at the level I was vibrating, which was low. I had low self-esteem (the weight most definitely contributed to that) and low self-worth. Again, copping to this helped me to make better choices about the men I allowed into my life. When I recognized this and took responsibility, I raised my own self-worth. Around the same time, I began to take care of my body physically, eating healthier and working out.

I learned that as an adult, no one will ever take responsibility for you except you. Taking responsibility for your life, your choices, and your experiences will be the biggest gift you can give yourself in the journey of getting to know yourself. Not all gifts come with giant bows; sometimes the best gifts come through hard, gritty honesty with yourself. I think it is kind of a funny thing—once you start to change one aspect of your life, you have to start changing all aspects of your life. It's like you can't be epic in one area and not the others. By taking responsibility, you own your life and your choices. No one and nothing can mess with you when you stand in alignment with your past, present, and future choices. It's empowerment at its most empowered.

COMMITMENT TO PURPOSE

The third strong choice I made—and one I couldn't have made without first having gone through the first and second strong choices—was to create my message and build my brand. For those of you who are creatives, you will wholeheartedly understand when I say that the hardest part of creating is sitting down to do so. Knowing that I was to write and share my experiences and lessons, I had to make the strong choice to commit to building the content, essentially from scratch.

Building anything requires tenacity. It requires a very strong core belief in oneself. It's understanding that your message or product will uplift and change the world. When you are creating such a thing, you have to put your ego aside to get it done. Building anything is hard work, period. I quickly learned that the amount of time and energy, elation mixed with frustration, and clarity mixed with confusion are why many people don't even start. I didn't want to be one of those people. I wanted to create and share my message with the world as I felt it to be important. I knew it was going to be hard work but I accepted that and I moved forward anyway.

I had already started a writing practice but it was more like I was writing when I felt like it, not so much like I was writing to turn it into my profession, my purpose. I picked up the book *The War of Art* by Steven Pressfield. If you are a creative and have not read this book, do yourself a favor and grab it ASAP. This book taught me the difference between an amateur and a professional and it's profoundly simple. It's the choice to sit down and do the work every day.

I realized that if I could create a yoga practice for myself, then I could create a writing practice for myself (they say the real yoga is off the mat anyhow). I wasn't fully committed to it until I *made the choice* to be. I had to get clear on my intention, making sure that my actions matched my intention. My intention was to write my stories to help people. However, I couldn't say I was a writer and not have documents upon documents to prove it. I had to sit down and write these stories to become a writer just like I had to show up on my yoga mat to become a yogi. This goes back to how you do one thing is how you do everything. I wanted to be in the utmost integrity with my life's purpose, so I made the strong choice to fully commit to my writing, my purpose.

The fun thing about being a creative is that you have a certain perspective of seeing how the Universe also creates. It's a partnership where you sit down and produce your work while allowing the Universe to bring you the other parts that help get your work out into the world. The more you understand about creation in general, the more you align to a higher energy, grasping that you get to consciously create all of your life. How cool is that? No, really!? We're in charge of our thoughts and our choices which ultimately lead to the kind of life we live.

If there's anything you take away from this chapter, let it be to understand that every choice you make is either going to uplift you or drain you. It will take time to decipher which is which. The easiest way to understand strong choices is asking yourself the questions, "Does this choice move me forward on the path toward my goals, or does it move me back?" and, "Is this a choice that aligns with my version of self-love?" It is a strong choice to actively work on yourself to improve your life. Please honor yourself in doing so.

CHAPTER FIVE

Patterns and Practices

In the ultimate honoring of my sacredness, I began to focus on my writing. I wholeheartedly knew I needed to share my message with the world—it was my purpose. I made the strong choice to make my writing a priority just like I had done with my yoga practice. With that in mind, I had to figure out exactly how to schedule it into my life, creating a pattern and practice of it.

Creating patterns and practices in your life is an exercise in understanding your choices. For much of my early life, my schedule was dictated for me: school, homework, dance classes, singing lessons, clubs, and committees. Every moment of each day was filled. Then in my twenties, my schedule was dictated by my work, which varied from day to day. My priority was to do whatever the work was to get paid, which often meant I didn't have a firm schedule, including my sleep schedule. I didn't really see my life as a series of choices, rather just random things that I did to keep myself afloat. The daily grind, if you will.

However, we all already have patterns and practices. From the basics of sleeping and brushing our teeth to checking e-mails for work, everything we do is a pattern and a practice. To fully grasp my own already non-consciously created patterns and practices, I had to learn the difference between unhealthy choices and healthy choices in all aspects of my life. I began to study which things were being done on autopilot mode and which things I did out of intention. I then made the strong choice to consciously re-create my patterns and practices—with intention, reflecting my healthiest self. My self-loving self.

LAPTOP LIFESTYLE

Around age twenty-six, I moved into a beautiful house with my boyfriend. We had an extra room and although I did not work from home at that time, I wanted to create an office space. My intention in creating the home office was that I eventually wanted to work from home. It took about a year for it to fully manifest, but once I hit my Saturn return, I had a shift in the way that I worked. Laptop lifestyle was becoming trendier and the work I was doing was mostly from my computer, so I started working from home. My intention had blossomed.

Working from home meant I didn't really have a set schedule, other than the few days a month where I had to be somewhere for work such as the occasional on-set day or a lunch meeting. Not having a set 9 to 5 schedule was ideal for me. It meant I could do my spiritual practices while most people were in morning traffic. It meant I could run errands while most people were at their offices. It meant I could go to yoga classes at 4:15 PM. It meant that I had been given the gift of time to write, while still working a job to pay my bills.

In my freedom-filled flexible schedule, some days were very productive and other days, not so much. On those less accomplished days, I would get frustrated with myself knowing that I had essentially wasted time. Sometimes it was good old-fashioned procrastination and other times it was poor time management (which can often be the same thing). Eventually, I realized that I was in charge of whether I would have a productive day or not, and that it was up to me to make the choice to schedule out my time.

I firmly believe that most people are not *busy,* rather, most people are unorganized and unprioritized. We all have the same exact 24 hours in the day and it's up to us to use them how we wish to. I wanted to conquer my time management so when I sat down to figure out exactly how to schedule a steady pattern and practice of writing into my life, I decided to schedule *everything* in my iCal.

My ideal day was scheduled like this:

7–8 AM: Arise from a restful, eight-hour night of sleep. Meditate, journal, and make my morning tea.

8–9 AM: Talk to one of my close friends/mentors for our daily touch base. Set an intention after our inspirational conversation. Make a protein shake.

9–11 AM: E-mails, calls and work for my "money job," the job that pays me.

11 AM–12 PM: Shower and get ready to leave the house.

12–3:30 PM: Go to my favorite coffee shop to eat and write (while still having access to my e-mails and phone in case something came up for my money job).

3:30–6:30 PM: Yoga (with **#traffuck**). While in the car, I would call my mom, sister, and other friends that I needed to catch up with. Or I would listen to inspirational podcasts.

6:30–8 PM: Dinner (sometimes with a friend, other times at home).

8–10 PM: Wind down the day, finishing up e-mails and prepping for the following day.

10 PM: "Bougie" bath with a book (bougie bath includes salts, oils, and crystals).

11 PM: Sleep.

That being said, I had to become extremely flexible with this. On some days, I wouldn't make it to the coffee shop at all. Instead, I'd be home all day because my money job required more from me on that day (keeping the roof over my head is obviously just as much of a priority as my writing is). On other days, I didn't make it to yoga because I ended up staying at the coffee shop longer as I was in a wonderful flow with my words. Regardless, I was now in charge of the choice of how I spent my time.

The biggest commitment I made to myself was to write no less than two paragraphs a day. *Every single day.* The only days I gave myself a pass were the days I was sick or when I was traveling (however, I find plane time to be a great time to write). Ninety percent of the time, those two paragraphs turned into two-plus pages. That's one of the secrets to success—wholeheartedly committing to an attainable daily goal that moves you one step closer to the desired outcome. This became my pattern and practice. It takes a million steps to build something, but unless you're taking a step each day (no matter the size of the step) and taking it one step at a time, it doesn't get built. Success should never be judged on the final outcome; success should be acknowledged in all of the active steps taken toward your goal.

This was *my* life I was creating—no one was going to write my stories for me—so I took it very seriously. I became obsessed by choice, investing in the *Field of Dreams* affirmation, "If you build it, they will come." Taking control of my time—managing it very consciously—was a strong choice to put myself and my sacred work as a priority. Putting yourself and your sacred work as a priority is an act of self-love.

SET YOURSELF UP FOR SUCCESS

I believe that to fully commit to your schedule, you also have to make the choice to give yourself all you need in order to succeed, consciously setting yourself up for success. This means making sure your environment supports you. Your environment includes many aspects of your life. It means your physical environment (both the space around you along with your actual body), your social environment, and your mental environment.

It became very clear to me that I needed to treat my body with the utmost respect for it to fully function if I was going to show up and produce my work every day. When I am sweating (working out) and eating properly (organically), my body works properly. I am clear-headed, I sleep eight full hours, I don't have nutzo cravings, and I have a firmer grasp on my to-do list.

Most people have FOMO (fear of missing out) while I have FOMS (fear of missing sleep). I know for a fact that I function at my best when I have a full eight hours. I chose to go to bed every night at the same time so that I was sure to get my eight hours. I even invested in high-quality bedding and sleep attire because I enjoy feeling luxurious. I also enjoy using a sleep mask to block off any window light—the darker the room, the deeper my sleep. Always invest in anything that makes you feel like a better version of yourself—it's an investment in *you*. I sometimes make the exception of going to bed a little later if I have an evening event or something of importance going on, however, I find if I go to sleep past midnight, my body knows when it's 7 AM and wakes up anyway, and on those days, I am not at my best.

The same goes for my nutrition routine. If I indulge in pizza (or any other carb-loaded fiesta), my body takes extra time to digest, making me sluggish. Also, it's the same situation with my workout routine. If I slack off on my workouts, my body isn't releasing the endorphins that keep me feeling upbeat. Not to say I don't indulge in pizza from time to time, but I do it very consciously, prepared for how it will affect me.

Knowing that I needed to feel alive and thriving to produce my work, this also meant nixing alcohol. In my twenties, I would partake in social drinking because it's just what people do, right? I had finally begun to respect my body by feeding it healthy foods and getting my sweat on, so I had to think long and hard about why I would make the choice to put something in my body that wasn't going to benefit me. When I really started looking at my life and my previous choices, it got me thinking. I realized that I did not even enjoy drinking. Like most, the older I got, the worse the hangover became. Honestly, my experience drinking was never really worth enduring the hangover. My purpose of writing and producing my work became far more important to me than partaking in a social poison that would lower my vibe for 24 to 48 hours afterward, killing my precious creative energy and time. I'll still toast with champagne at a wedding or have a nice glass of wine curated with a lovely meal, but those times are few and far between, and there is always a special occasion intention involved. I sometimes think about how we view Ernest Hemingway writing with a drink in hand. Then I remember that he shot himself.

Choosing to take care of my health was a huge part of controlling my time management. The things I want to do in my life and create for the world require me to be in tip-top shape—mentally, physically, and emotionally. Bottom line, when my body works properly, I am able to produce my best work.

Even if you don't have some sort of project or goal that you're aligning your health and wellness with, it's still imperative to put yourself first. If no one has ever given you the permission to put yourself first, here—I'm giving you the go-ahead. You're allowed to put yourself first, making yourself your number-one priority. So many of us, especially women, end up taking care of everyone else before we tend to ourselves. Don't leave yourself behind! It's airplane safety 101—put on your oxygen mask first before helping others. When you take care of your body, you take care of your sacredness.

CONSCIOUSLY ANTI-SOCIAL

If you've been my friend over the last few years, pretty much the only time we spent together was at yoga, then occasionally, we'd grab a quick bite to eat, doing a quick catch-up on life. Then I'd head back into my writing cave. I made the choice to put my social life on the back burner. I used all of my free time—including all hours of the weekends—to create my projects and take care of myself.

I would get phone calls from friends that pretty much went like this:

Friend: "I'm in your neighborhood . . . want to grab a coffee?"

Heather: "Thanks for calling, so great to hear from you! I'm in the middle of writing but perhaps we can meet for a yoga class later this week?"

Or:

Friend: "Do you want to go out on Saturday night to grab drinks?"

Heather: "I'd love to see you but I'm not available Saturday night. Perhaps we can grab a meal on Tuesday evening after my yoga class?"

I overcame the peer pressure and maintained my friendships by offering other opportunities to share time together that better served me. My friends were happy to join me at yoga then grab a bite to eat, with most of them understanding that I was working on myself and my art, my purpose.

The friends that didn't understand soon fell out of the picture (more on that in a future chapter).

MINDFUL MATING

Putting my social life on the back burner also meant no worthless dating. I only had to go on one "forced" date to know it wasn't for me. By forced, I mean society-driven peer pressure. About a year after my breakup, I got on a dating app because it's what people do, right? I talked to a few guys through messaging and most of them were shockingly honest about just wanting sex. Once that confession came out, I would stop conversing with them. I was in a message discussion with a man who was polite and interested in meeting for lunch. I thought, "Sure, why not?" Again, because that's what people do, right?

We met for lunch. He was kind but there was zero spark and we had very little in common. The conversation wasn't even worth trying to build a friendship. As I was having this experience, it dawned on me that this was a giant waste of my time. I would have rather been home working on my projects, using my time wisely.

I had only signed up for a dating app as that's "what people do." It wasn't something my intuition called me to do. I was operating from a place of societal norm along with fear from others. I would often hear:

"You're now in your thirties! Don't you want to have kids?"

"How are you going to meet someone if you're not out there in the game pool?"

"Tech dating is the modern way."

As someone who worked so hard to get off of the hamster wheel of societal norm, a dating app was never going to work for me—especially when my intuition wasn't calling me toward it. I had enough trust that the Universe would align me with my perfect partner when it was time. Finding love with a compatible person is something that can't be forced. Plus, my focus was on creating and writing, not dating, so I made the strong choice to fully commit to my work, knowing that I would not be alone forever, contrary to popular societal beliefs.

For me to align with the kind of man that I wanted to share my life with, I had to build a firm foundation for not only my projects but for my sacredness, as well. My choice to create patterns and practices while writing was part of setting up my foundation of my own self-love. I learned more about myself while exploring my daily patterns and practices, essentially understanding more of my identity. My definition of self-love is a righteous knowing of one's identity. It dawned on me when I made the choice to no longer mindlessly date that I needed to fully know how to love myself so that I could allow a man to love me the way that I desired and deserved to be loved.

STRONG FOUNDATION

Eventually, as I continued to build out my foundation and my body of written work, it was time for me to emerge into the world of social events again. It took me nearly two years of cave time before I was ready to present my work. But when I did emerge, people were shocked. Not that I started socializing again, but at the fact that I had written so much content and had a plethora of thoroughly polished ideas to present. I came to meetings beyond prepared. I had done the work.

One producer told me that I had built out my brand and accomplished more than some of the producers he'd worked with on big-budget productions. I asked him, "If that's the case, then how do these people work if they don't *do* the work?"

His reply was simple, "Well, they work that one time, but usually never again."

It was clear to me that the work I was bringing into the world was going to sustain itself. I had taken two years out of my social life to devote my time to create the foundation for the rest of my life. I was actually in awe of myself once I viewed it from this perspective. When you put in the hard work to build a strong foundation—in all areas of your life—it's the combination of thoughts plus choices plus actions which can only equal success. (Side note: sometimes success arrives after many setbacks, but please don't give up! Your dream is worth the work to conquer it!)

COMMITMENT TO THE PROCESS

Everything is a choice, and you make better choices by implementing patterns and practices. Self-love is nothing more than a commitment to the process. Whatever process you are going through—whether work/project based, spiritual growth, health and wellness goals, relationships with others—you have to commit to it fully.

Life on Earth is a repetition. The sun rises and sets every day. The moon phases itself through a monthly cycle. The seasons change every three months. The year repeats its twelve-month cycle annually. Create your life in repetition to see results. This isn't to say that you can't be spontaneous and have fun—please, do have fun with your life! Yet do things consciously. Know when you choose to go on a vacation to leave your work at home, committing fully to the present moment, just as you commit fully to the present moment at work.

You can be a creature of habit or you can be a creator of habit (self-love is the latter). Give yourself the opportunity to learn the difference between your unhealthy choices and healthy choices. Then stop making the unhealthy ones. Period. I know it's easier said than done, but truth bomb: if you want to live the life of your dreams, then you have to have full awareness of your choices.

> **You can be a creature of habit or you can be a creator of habit (self-love is the latter).**

Breaking a bad habit is simply making the choice to do so. They say it takes twenty-one days to fully incorporate a new routine into your life. Take those twenty-one days and replace the bad habit with a good habit. Transform the previous patterns that limit you from becoming the best version of yourself. Yes, this is a discipline. It becomes easier with a committed practice.

Here's the good thing about the word practice—it's just that. A practice. And, practice makes perfect. Which means while practicing finding what works for you, you get to experiment with all sorts of different trials which will eventually lead you to your perfect pattern, the one that you personally designed—the one that works best for you. Consciously creating healthy patterns and practices helps to break the chaotic infinity loop that has held you captive on your hamster wheel. Once you create your patterns and practices, you create your own life.

Self-love is a practice which eventually becomes a pattern. Self-love is understanding your boundaries. You get to learn about your personal boundaries when actively making strong choices while creating patterns and practices. Self-love is where choices meet actions that are in alignment with one another. Making good choices while creating patterns and practices is the key to attaining and sustaining not only self-love, but the exact life you want to live.

Let's break this down one more time so we're totally clear:

1. Make strong choices: choices that serve your growth and your sacredness.

2. Create patterns and practices. Find the discipline to commit to the life *you* want to live. No one is going to do this for you and P.S., most successful people are not smarter per se, rather they're just disciplined in their work.

3. Go love yourself by implementing your choices, patterns, and practices into your daily life.

4. Wash, rinse, repeat.

Do the Work

Now that we've gone over some of the physical work to cultivate self-love, let's discuss more in-depth about the inner work required—specifically your thoughts. If you can't control what you think, you can't control what you do. When you learn to control and maneuver your thoughts, you learn how to control and maneuver your life. With that truth bomb being dropped, we've got to dig deeper into our thoughts—more specifically—how our thoughts are creating our reality. Just like everything else in life, if you want something, you have to work for it—and the inner

> When you learn to control and maneuver your thoughts, you learn how to control and maneuver your life.

work—that is where the *real* work is done. This is where the seed of self-love spreads its roots. This is the where we cross over from self-development to soul-development.

THOUGHTS CREATE EXPERIENCES

I shared my story about my first vision board in chapter one and how I ended up 1,000 feet away from the Hollywood sign.

This is one of a million wonderful, beautiful things that I have manifested with my thoughts creating the experiences in my life. However, I want to share a personal story where a negative thought created a negative experience to show the dichotomy.

In Judaism, *Heshbon Ha-Nefesh* is the period leading up to Rosh Hashanah (the Jewish New Year) and Yom Kippur (Day of Atonement). Heshbon Ha-Nefesh is a time to reflect on any wrongs you may have committed in the previous year. The final ten days, the space between Rosh Hashanah and Yom Kippur, called *Teshuva*, are designated to actively make amends to anyone you may have wronged so that you can move forward into Yom Kippur with a clean slate.

During a recent Heshbon Ha-Nefesh, I spent time thinking about my actions over the previous year. I went about my normal practices—mindfulness, meditation, daily journal, gratitude journal, yoga—I do a lot of reflection work on the regular, so this didn't really impact me too much. Honestly, I couldn't find anyone or anything that I needed to apologize to or for. One of the things that my self-love journey has taught me is to own up to my mistakes instantly, not letting them sit and brew in avoidance. Anything I had done wrong, I had already copped to. I felt clear, or at least I thought I did. We were halfway into the Teshuva period when I realized that maybe there was one person that I needed to make amends with.

I had been submitting my work to publishers and producers, with the intention of aligning with the right people who could help me on my next steps of getting my work out into the world. I got an e-mail response from a publisher that I had set my high hopes on. It was a rejection letter and it sent me spinning: "Why doesn't this person like it? How can I make it better for them? I need to do/be better."

I decided I was going to take my flustered frustration and literally spin it out, as sweating problems out via a strong workout can be a cathartic way to process emotions. My best friend Hunter had given me a spin bike for my apartment a few months prior. We put it in the corner, next to my bookshelf (because where else do you put a spin bike in a one-bedroom apartment?). I remember the day he installed it, he told me, "Don't go too fast, you'll get hurt." I sat down and started pedaling. Faster. Harder. Twisting the resistance up further, I was determined to clear my frustration.

The harder I went at it, the most frustrated I got. Inevitably, my left foot slipped out as the speeding pedal scraped up my entire shin, instantly gashing it open. As Hunter had warned me, I went too fast and I got hurt. I leaned over against the bookshelf to find my balance when Louise Hay's *You Can Heal Your Life* came tumbling down.

I got off the bike, yelling curse words, wobbling over to my kitchen to grab some towels to clean up the blood. And then I fell to the floor, where I started crying. I was having a Breakdown to Breakthrough (in the kitchen, yet again). Except I realized I wasn't crying about the quite literal bloody pain, I was crying to release all the stress I had put on myself. It hit me in that moment that the person I needed to make amends with was *me*.

A moment of deep, vulnerable honesty between me, myself, and I: I can be *really* hard on myself. I needed to be more compassionate toward myself. I needed to apologize to myself for all I've put myself through. I sat there on the kitchen floor and cried for a while, letting the emotions flow through me. The human experience is an emotional experience. I actually really enjoy the process of emoting through tears. It's a purge, a rebirth, which always clears the path and expands my soul growth. Allowing my feelings to come forward and facing them head-on ended up being far more cathartic than sweating them out on the bike.

I had been betraying my sacredness. I was essentially pushing myself both in my projects and on the bike, not listening to messages from my Higher Self, my intuition. Your intuition is always trying to tell you everything you need to know. Your intuition is your connection to the higher power. I had lost sight of this, forgetting to trust in the Universe and trust in the process. I wasn't listening. I was disconnected.

All of the work I was creating was taking time, and as we know from history, empires aren't built in day. I realized I needed to chill out. Under the "Build it and they will come" strategy, I had zero to worry about. The Universe will inevitably align me with the right publishers and producers when it's time. *Ahh*, it wasn't time yet. I needed to learn yet another lesson—patience. It was no surprise to me that this happened during the High Holidays—I truly believe divine timing is always at play. The energies were just right for me to experience—and understand—a Breakdown to Breakthrough.

The hard thoughts that I had about myself had manifested in this Breakdown to Breakthrough. The metaphor translated to speeding up was not helping—speeding up literally hurt me. I needed to slow down. I reached over to look up the physical ailments that I had just experienced in *You Can Heal Your Life.*

- Wounds essentially mean that one has anger toward the self.

- Shin issues relate to the breaking down of ideals.

Okay Teshuva, you won this round. Although I truly believe that I needed to have this breakdown to be able to break through to rise to my next level, my hard-on-myself thoughts certainly contributed to the bloody experience. I will carry the scar on my left shin for the rest of my life, but it's my own personal war-with-myself-wound, reminding me that all thoughts create all experiences.

INNER DIALOGUE

I had been unkind toward myself in regard to my rejection letter. I went right into the negative. "Why doesn't this person like it? How can I make it better for them? I need to do/ be better." Now looking back at it, a healthier and kinder thought would have been, "This is not the right person to align with. The Universe will send me a better match." While I eventually got to that point, I would have rather gotten there faster, sans the scar.

In order to love yourself, you must have a loving inner dialogue. You have to treat yourself with love and this starts in your very own thoughts. This requires digging deep, discovering where the root of your thoughts come from (hint: it's often found in our upbringings or from a traumatic event that we've held on to in our subconscious). This kind of work undoubtedly takes time. It's an unfolding of learning about yourself, layer by layer. Honestly, I'm still learning about and unpeeling my layers and I will probably be doing so for my entire life, uncovering new lessons and jumping to new levels as I continue to grow.

Understanding your previous choices, patterns, and practices will unveil to you where your thoughts stem from.

Just as we all already have ingrained physical patterns and practices such as brushing our teeth and checking e-mails, we also have ingrained thought patterns and practices. Most people live their entire lives on autopilot, stuck in their own chaotic infinity loop of repeated thoughts. For some people, it's an insanity loop if their thoughts are negative.

Mindfulness is one of those trending and overused words floating around out there right now in the yoga and self-help world. However, mindfulness is the way to break the chain of the chaotic infinity loop. But what exactly *is* mindfulness?

In my own personal experience, my mindfulness strengthened when I started my yoga practice. While I have always been someone who is sensitive to energy and situations, when I began doing yoga on a regular basis, I became very aware of my thoughts. One of my very favorite teachers—Sarah Ezrin—said something during a class one day that stuck with me. We were in *Ardha Chandrasana,* or half moon pose. In this pose, you have one arm down on the ground in front of you, one leg stretched out back behind you in the air, one leg standing and rooting you down on the ground, and one arm flying high above you in the air. You have to find the balance between the arm and leg that are rooted down while simultaneously soaring high with the arm and leg that are air bound. This pose requires some thought to get into and also to hold. Sarah said, "You can only think about being here in this pose right now. If your mind goes elsewhere, you will lose your balance and fall over."

Mindfulness is being present with your thoughts, your actions, and also your feelings. When we're not mindful, we lose our balance.

I am a huge fan of self-reflection, clearly. I often get

asked, "How can one be present, being in the moment, and still do reflective work?" It does seem a little oxymoronic, however, I find it imperative to look back in order to move forward with clarity. Looking back to analyze your previous choices, including thought patterns—the good and the bad—allows you to see yourself for who you were at that point, who you are right now, and who you want to become.

The willingness to look back to figure out where you came from—understanding the seed of your thought patterns—is a huge step to changing your habits and way of life. All of your thoughts have created all of your experiences; previous, present, and future. If you are not pleased with some of your experiences, you need to analyze your past thoughts and actions—your choices—so that you learn from them. Analyzing is the first step out of the chaotic infinity loop. It is a strong choice to do this work and worthy of a pat on the back. (Seriously, pat yourself on the back. Most people don't even have the courage to pick up these kinds of books.)

It became clear to me in my mid-twenties that my parents' thought patterns about money were ingrained in me. A lot of our parents' thought patterns about life naturally become ingrained in us as it's what we know and what we see while we're growing up. Our little spongy minds soak up everything from our early environments. To be very clear, I grew up extremely blessed. There was always a roof over my head, a warm bed to sleep in, food in the fridge, new clothes, shoes, and backpacks every fall, and many dance classes and singing lessons to attend. Yet, my little ears often overheard conversations about how there wasn't enough money. But clearly, there was enough since we never went without.

The day I had eight dollars left in my bank account and

spent seven of them on the latte that got me my next job, I had the epiphany that I was always taken care of. This is where I chose to shift the story in my head so it would serve me better. I had never gone without—regardless if the funds came from family, credit, loans, or my own work. There has always been enough money and there always will be enough money.

This epiphany not only showed me how to trust the Universe, but it also sparked a self-reflective journey to my childhood regarding money. I thought back to everything I could remember in regard to finances. I love my parents and they are wonderfully kind people, but I knew I needed to clear the financial karma that had been ingrained in me. This was a seed that I wanted to uproot since it no longer served me. I had to dispose of their inner dialogue that had been impressed onto me and replace it with my own inner dialogue which reflected how I wanted to view money.

I began to work on my thoughts coming into alignment with a positive intention. Anytime I had a negative thought regarding my own finances, I would quickly take note of the thought and change it immediately. To change my thought, I would counteract it with an affirmation of my abundance: "I am financially self-sufficient."

If you take nothing from this book except for one thing, please take this:

> The trick to overcoming a negative thought is to counteract it with a positive affirmation. Then, do a physical action that affirms the affirmation, showing the Universe that you have faith and trust in the bigger plan, and—most importantly—that you believe in yourself!

The action I took to affirm my affirmation was kind of silly but go with me on this one. I went to the Dollar Store and purchased some play money. I got 1,000 play dollars for one U.S. dollar! What a deal, right? To change my thought patterns and practices, each time I would have a negative thought about money, I counteracted it with the positive affirmation. Then I would take one of my play money bills and deposit it into a piggy bank. I knew it wasn't a "real" deposit but the action is what mattered. I believed in my abundance. I believed in my hard work to change my thoughts. Honestly, it doesn't matter what kind of action you take—silly or not. Find an action that works for you. The metaphor of play money worked for me and most importantly, it made me feel better because I was actively tackling my negative thought issues.

When you decide to take a journey down memory lane to discover where the seeds of your thoughts are buried, do so without judgment. Identifying your weakness is not for, well, the weak. What happened in the past are just facts, not life sentences. Accept everything as part of your history and move forward without judgment. Have self-compassion (please don't injure your shin on a spin bike because you're mentally beating the crap out of yourself, pushing *too* hard). Know that it's a courageous choice to take the journey. Be present by allowing yourself to analyze the past but do not get stuck there. Identify the thought patterns that hold you back then rearrange the thoughts to serve you better—release the old to make room for the new. I love the metaphor of cleaning out your closet, letting go of all the old clothes that you no longer wear so that you make room to fill it with new clothes. Use this metaphor for your thoughts—releasing the negative ones to make room for the positive ones. Overcoming your negative thoughts is the only way to live a positive life.

Sometimes this kind of inner work analyzing your issues requires some extra help. Seek a mentor or a therapist if needed. Write in a journal to help process your self-evaluations. Have deep conversations about your journey with a friend you trust. Find a creative way to express yourself—through art, painting, dancing, music—and release your emotions to fly free. Finding a safe way to process your thoughts, feelings, and emotions will help you in this very sacred and intimate journey of getting to know—and fall in love with—yourself. Pulling up the overgrown negative thought weeds and replanting healthy seeds in your metaphorical thought garden can only lead to beautifully blooming thoughts. Give yourself the gift of fertile grounds where you can grow the life you wish to live.

> **Overcoming your negative thoughts is the only way to live a positive life.**

MESSY SPACE EQUALS MESSY THOUGHTS

A few years back when I was actively discovering what self-love looked like and meant to me, I was often found in yoga classes, processing my mind, body, and spirit. One time, I went to grab my yoga props from the back of the room, prepping for class. When I got back to my mat, I put my block strategically up to the right of my mat and my bolster over to the left of my mat. This was where I liked them to be placed as it's easy for me to reach over to grab when needed during certain poses. Then a thought occurred: "Your outer surroundings are a direct reflection of your inner thoughts."

That moment allowed me to relate my physical space to my inner space. This thought helped me shift into a deeper metaphor, making it a light bulb, *aha* moment for me. I went home that day and started looking at my physical space. Overall, I'm fairly organized and clean, however, sometimes I can let my to-file pile go untouched for weeks at a time. I began to think about my epiphany of outer surroundings reflecting my inner thoughts. If I had a pile of unorganized papers sitting in front me, I probably had a pile of unorganized thoughts within me. I sat down and started sorting through the pile. I felt so much better when I was done.

I come back to this metaphor often. I consciously work on keeping my space very clean and organized, and I take notice when that pile appears again (because it will always inevitably appear again—life is an ebb and flow). Not everyone's pile of unorganized papers will be a matching metaphor for their thoughts, but this is what worked for me and is a reminder of when I need to step up my game. Usually, when the pile appears, I sit down and clean it up, then I think about my thoughts and where I may have been slacking off on my inner work.

My desk mess gives me the opportunity—a practice—to consciously create better conditions for myself. By creating patterns and practices, you are actively taking control of your energy and vibration. *Energy* and *vibration* are fancy-schmancy spiritual words that I touched on earlier in Chapter three. There are much more complex ways to explore this (if you'd like to dig deeper, listen to Abraham Hicks on YouTube) but I'm going to break it down simply.

Energy is a vibration. *You* are energy. You are in a vibration (ranging from low to high). When your thoughts are negative, you are in a low vibration. When your thoughts are positive, you are in a high vibration. Your thoughts control your vibration. When you can control your thoughts, you can control your life. *Capisce?*

Self-love is the ultimate knowing of one's identity. When you know and understand your thoughts, you get to consciously create your life, mapping out your own directions. Your path, your map.

FORGIVENESS

We typically know what gets us in our positive vibrations—joy from doing something we love, laughter shared with friends, feeling hopeful when we wake up and the sun is shining. We all know the happy, as we have all had moments of joy. Happiness is a choice. Sometimes happiness takes time to cultivate as you have to dig deep to remove anything that's in your energy—your thoughts—that might be holding you back from a higher and happier vibration.

First and foremost, we all have had our fair share of mishaps and mistakes. Even the things that you think are previous mistakes are not mistakes. These incidents are for your growth path. Everything happens *for* you, not *to* you. What you may view as "bad things" that have happened in your life are actually things that you needed to experience so you could learn from them. The Universe is a beautiful tapestry; everything is woven together as it should be.

Many of us bury and submerge our past experiences, "let bygones be bygones" if you will. However, when you bury these experiences (ahem: emotions) without properly processing them, they will inevitably creep into your life, thoughts, and vibrations, causing more pain than necessary. Anger, secrets, shame, and fears that morph into unhealthy choices and self-sabotage—you name it—your very own insecure house of cards will always fall, somehow, someway. Fun fact: "Do the work" is slang for learning to understand your emotions. When you have emotional intelligence, you have the ability to conquer anything life throws at you.

My personal story of attempting to "let bygones be bygones" involves my former relationship—however, not him specifically. When we parted ways, it was very amicable. In other words, we consciously uncoupled before Gwyneth and Chris made it a trend. I went about my life, growing and exploring, finding my version of self-love—letting bygones be bygones in regard to him and the experiences that came with that relationship.

When I decided to begin writing, I had a strong urge to write about my relationships. I knew that it would be a cathartic experience and I would be able to analyze my previous choices, actions, patterns and practices in relation to how I did relationships. When I got to the chapter on this particular relationship, something unexpected happened.

David, playing the part of my editor, read all of my first drafts. I printed it out and handed it to him as I had done before with previous chapters. After he read it, he pointed to all of the other previous printouts of the other chapters saying, "Those, those over there . . . those are light. They are very funny. You have clearly processed all of those relationships. This one though, you didn't just lightly hand it over to me. This one hit with a thud. This is a giant brick of anger."

He was right. I was holding on to anger from my past relationship—however, it had very little to do with the actual man I was in a relationship with—rather it was the community he was from.

My ex is a Persian Jew from Los Angeles (otherwise known as "Tehrangeles"—if you're familiar with *The Shahs of Sunset*). I, not being a Persian Jew, was an instant outcast. While some of his family members treated me nicely, others were downright awful to me and all because I was different from them.

A little over a year into our relationship, he and I walked into the hotel where one of his extended family member's wedding was about to take place. The family said to me, "You look so pretty! . . . You can't sit with us."

I looked at my boyfriend, who then started speaking Farsi to his family. I had no idea what the words being spoken meant but I fully understood the situation. I was not welcome to sit at the family table because I was different. Even though I embodied other checklist qualities (kind, caring, educated, successful, classy, well put-together, empowered), I wasn't Persian. I didn't fit into their mold—or rather, the illusion they wanted to present to the public of what their "mold" appeared to be.

This is one of hundreds of situations that happened during the four years he and I spent together (and I did sit with my boyfriend at the family table because no one can tell this girl what or what not to do). There were a lot of similar situations that I nonchalantly tried to sweep under the Persian rug, not processing fully. Until that is, I wrote it all out in the giant brick of anger chapter which may as well have been titled, "Persian Aversion."

I went back into my writing cave to edit—and to also figure out how to cultivate forgiveness for all that I'd been through. I realized I had started judging not only my ex's family but the entire community. I would see a Persian person out and about (they're everywhere in L.A.) and I would have some sort of negative thought and/or judgment—and I didn't even know this person! I had built up a fence around me with a sign that clearly read, "No Persians Allowed."

As I went through my processing (editing draft after draft), I kept reminding myself that it had all happened *for* me, not *to* me. A few months later, I ran into someone I knew who was also a Persian Jew. When we saw each other, he was instantly all hugs and double Persian kisses. He was kind, providing me with a giant shield against my angry projection. He was the first Persian I had seen in over two years that I didn't instantly blast my inner anger toward.

I realized that I had created a destructive behavior toward the Persian community because I had closed off my heart. I had projected my anger out onto all Persians, as I viewed them all as people who would hurt me since I had been very specifically hurt by a select few in my past. I placed blame on the people that had hurt me when in reality I needed to take responsibility for my own healing. I had been suffering from my own thoughts about the experience I'd had. This realization was my first step in finding forgiveness. I also realized that suffering is a choice—everything comes down to how you choose to view it.

I went back into my writing cave to edit my Persian Aversion story—but this time, with a lighter, more open heart. Then, my story got funny. Finding the humor in all that had happened, processing through laughter, that's when I knew I'd reached forgiveness. When we elevate our energy enough to crack jokes about the things that previously hurt us, that's enlightenment (why do you think the Buddha is often pictured as laughing?).

I had to open up my heart, releasing all the shackled-up energy from my past pains. Most of the pain I had brought upon myself, just like my situation with the spin bike. The heavy stuff I was carrying, I had placed in my very own basket with my own thoughts and perspective. I not only had to forgive my past situations, I had to forgive myself for carrying useless and unnecessary baggage in my basket. And, you know what? I now have a handful of Persians that I consider dear friends, a few even close enough to call family. I had to purge my negative emotions to make space for positive ones to come in. I would have missed out on these beautiful friendships if I hadn't opened up my heart, releasing my own built-up anger. When your heart is open, you are free.

When something triggers you, take notice of it. Don't judge it or get mad at it. Your triggers are simply just pointing out what needs to be healed within you. Become aware of your triggers, your flaws, your insecurities, your fears, and your doubts. These aren't to be shoved under the rug—these are the things to dig deeper into, exploring why they exist within you in the first place. The answers you are seeking are deep down in these triggers. Become aware of them and honor them.

Forgiveness not only takes awareness but also time. It's something that's done in steps. It's done in steps because every step you take, you peel back another layer, uncovering another lesson, another epiphany. As I mentioned before, working on yourself takes time as emotions are so detailed and layered. Give yourself permission to "peel to heal." Just like onions, peeling sometimes brings on tears. Embrace them. You still keep chopping up that onion—regardless of the tears—because you need it for your meal, don't you? Peeling back your layers is doing the work required to get to your core to understand who you are. **#peeltoheal**

Know that no one is on the wrong path. You're right where you're supposed to be at all times, even if it is painful. The key to healing your past traumas is to embrace the pain; become friends with your pain so that you can understand it. When you understand the pain, it becomes familiar, manageable, and healable. If you push it under the proverbial rug, you'll inevitably trip on it.

Pain is the indicator that there's a lesson to be learned. The beauty of recognizing your pain is that you have the ability to heal it, which can change your life and be a course correct, setting you on a whole new beautiful path. When you heal your pain, your path becomes clearer. When you view life as everything is happening *for* you, not *to* you, you can then grasp your situations better. And, don't forget to have patience—be patient with yourself and the way things are unfolding and peeling (healing) in your life.

CHAPTER SEVEN

Intentions, Rituals, and Metaphors

We've covered a lot of deep and intense work thus far. Give yourself a pat on the back for making it through the hardest parts. These next few chapters are geared toward understanding the rituals you can create for yourself that are required to maintain a life filled with self-love. With many of us getting caught in our chaotic infinity loop, mindful intentions followed by rituals will help you to escape from it. Having intentions and rituals are where you can begin implementing, creating your daily blueprint for an excellent life. To live your best life, you have to understand your intentions, create your rituals, and honor your own personal metaphors.

INTENTIONS

To dig a bit deeper into the "thoughts create things" category, let's talk about intentions. An *intention,* by definition, is a "well-thought-out thought." When you have clear intentions, you have awareness of what you're doing. When you set an intention for yourself, situation, or experience, you create a *vibration*. The energy will then manifest according to the vibration back to the intention you set for yourself (in other words, it's all connected). Intentions relate back to strong choices—how you do one thing is how you do everything. One of my main intentions is to do everything wholeheartedly (because why do anything at all unless your heart is in it?). If your whole heart is not in it, that's your key to stay home and not participate.

During my time spent with my former boyfriend's Persian Jewish family, he, along with other family members, were under some sort of unspoken obligation to attend all Shabbats and High Holidays. The family peer pressure manifested as unhealthy guilt, which always created a miserable experience. When things are done out of guilt and/or obligation, there is zero lack of intention (not to mention integrity).

At many of these events, the elder generation would be the ones saying the prayers while the younger generation (by younger, I am referring to people in their twenties and thirties, in other words, fully grown adults) would talk and gossip over the entire prayer session. I always found this to be disrespectful. I mean, those were their grandparents, after all. I always walked away from these events irked because I believe that regardless if one practices the religion or not, respect is due to your elders. And, if you don't practice the religion and you're disrespecting your elders, then why even bother going? The disrespect isn't just to Grandpa, but even more so to yourself as you're not following your own heart. And, if you're not following your own heart, you don't know your intentions and you don't know yourself.

One year for a Passover Seder, my boss at that time invited us to her house. My then boyfriend and I decided to attend as we were looking for something with more meaning and less chatty gossip. This Seder was done with intention, going through the *Haggadah* (the stories of Moses and prayers associated with the holiday), and discussion around the table of what slavery and liberation meant not only thousands of years ago but how the topic is still relevant in today's day and age. At the end of the night as my boyfriend and I walked to the car, he said to me, "That was the best Jewish experience I've ever had. I didn't know half of the stories in the Haggadah and I certainly never thought to relate them to today's situations."

He hadn't realized things could be done differently because he had always done the family requirement out of guilt and obligation. He lacked intention and personal direction because he didn't realize he had a choice on how to participate in the religion of his upbringing. Once he had that experience, he began to craft his own meaningful rituals, filled with intentions. His intention was to create Jewish experiences that were impactful for him personally and still respectful to the family. His intention met his strong choice to do what was best for him.

Intention comes down to clarity. Clarity comes down to knowing yourself. Knowing yourself is the ultimate self-love. Are you noticing that all the topics we've gone over thus far interact with one another? Self-love incorporates many, many lessons that all reflect on one another (how you do one thing is how you do everything).

RITUALS

A *ritual*, by definition, is an "action or behavior that is regularly followed or performed." A ritual is also another name for patterns and practices of what you do with your day. While by definition you could call brushing your teeth a ritual, I choose to make the word ritual a bit more meaningful, relating it to strong choices in action. While some of my daily strong choices might seem mundane (maybe not quite as mundane as brushing my teeth), they are the things I do to help expand my spirituality. My rituals are sacred actions.

Earlier I listed my daily schedule that I crafted for myself to stay on top of my patterns and practices. Some of those tasks included doing the physical work to get paid along with my dedication to my craft which I aimed to turn into a career. Other tasks included my sacred actions, my rituals. I believe it's important to have a balance of what I call "human work" (the stuff that keeps you alive, like work that pays the bills, and things like doing laundry and washing dishes) and the "spiritual work." When it's scheduled out, you're more likely to perform all of the patterns and practices, along with the rituals.

I consider the act of making my morning tea a ritual. I learned about tea and the ritual of it from a boss who introduced me to the entire world of tea (which I became healthily obsessed with). Up until then, I had only had sweet tea (Southern girl right here). I had never really done high tea or teas for health reasons (clearly sweet tea is not consumed for the health benefits). Making my morning tea became a ritual because it's a daily action which I then follow by journaling. Each morning after my tea has been made, I sit down with my journal. Sometimes it's my "what's happening in my life" journal and other times it's a gratitude journal where I list out all the things I'm grateful for (caffeinated tea has made the list more than once). My journaling may include creating a new manifestation list or digging through my thoughts on something that's been bugging me which clearly needs to be understood so I can release it to heal. Regardless of whatever I'm penning down, I sit with my thoughts and my cup of tea.

Sometimes I'll do a guiding journaling practice, such as *The Magic* by Rhonda Byrne or *The Lotus and the Lily* by Janet Conner. Participating in each of these practices is a month-long process. They help me to focus on one specific topic (*The Magic* is for gratitude, *The Lotus and the Lily* is about forgiveness and healing, leading up to manifestation), while keeping me accountable to show up to my journaling page daily since both practices are formulated within a scheduled month. When I'm not working on a guided journal practice, I'll alternate to a fiction book because I love letting a story take me away to another life momentarily. Fiction invokes my creativity. I actively have to remind myself that it's okay to take a break from the deep spiritual work and dive into some fun every now and then.

When I worked in the mall in my early twenties, I was right next door to the Godiva store. Every Tuesday, I noticed a woman who appeared to be in her eighties go into Godiva and come out a few minutes later with a treat. One day, she came into the store I worked at to buy a lipstick and I asked her about her Tuesdays with Godiva. She said, "I treat myself to a chocolate-covered strawberry every week. While married to my husband, he would bring me chocolate-covered strawberries every week, for forty-five years. When he passed away a few years ago, I saw no reason not to continue the ritual. If you don't treat yourself, no one else will." This story has stayed with me since the day I heard it over twelve years ago. It's stayed with me so much so that I created a ritual to treat myself to fresh flowers weekly.

My writing became a ritual. My yoga practice became a ritual. My bougie baths became a ritual. My bougie sleeping habits became a ritual. Treating myself to fresh flowers became a ritual. I crafted out my daily life to become a series of intentions, strong choices, patterns and practices, and rituals—expanding my mind, body, and spirit. All of these themes helped me create clarity about who I am and the life I want to live. These things also brought moments of joy to me. When choice meets action while making a daily routine of things that are filled with self-love and self-care, your overall energy will shift, causing your quality of life to skyrocket.

Tea, journaling, and yoga are a few of my "mind and body" rituals. Let's discuss spiritual rituals—like what exactly is meditation?

My former boyfriend would sit and meditate daily for hours. Sometimes he would have on Hindu Kirtan music, chanting along to the Sanskrit mantras. At the time, I had no idea how he did it over and over, every single day. I'd want to spend time with him and he'd be meditating. I'd want to watch a movie and he'd be blasting Sanskrit mantras. I remember thinking that if this is what meditation is, I didn't want anything to do with it. Now in hindsight, I can see that it was his spiritual ritual—and who was I to judge what worked for him? It wasn't until the last few years on my own that I realized meditation didn't necessarily mean that I had to sit in lotus position, close my eyes for an hour, and chant to a deity (although I've certainly said my fair share of worthy *Om Gumgana Pataya Namahas* during my years in the yoga world).

Meditation is about one thing and one thing only: your breath. It doesn't matter if you tune into your breath through sitting in lotus position or if you do it while in yoga. You can literally do anything you want to do while meditating as long as you are focused on your breathing. I had a bad taste in my mouth about meditation until I decided to give it a new spin. I've always been able to zone into a different energetical space through music. Music makes my vibration expand. I feel higher and connected when listening to music. When I discovered binaural beats, I realized that was my way of removing the block I had about meditation, making it a more real, pliable action that related to the twenty-first century.

Binaural beats are an auditory illusion perceived when two tones in lower frequencies essentially bounce between ear to ear (you wear headphones to listen), creating more harmony in your brain, allowing you to relax and reach a meditative state. At night after my bougie bath, I snuggle into bed and put on my headphones. Sometimes, I have a more specific intention going on in my head if it's been a particularly stressful day—such as "breathe in peace, breathe out stress"—matching my intentional words with my breath. Often, I drift off to sleep within a few minutes of putting on my headphones. I enjoy this practice as it instantly calms me down, preparing me for a night of sleep so I can wake up well-rested.

There are other practices you can do to achieve a calmer state of mind. Anything you find cathartic will work. There are zen sand gardens, journaling, drawing, yin yoga, reiki—whatever you find that works for you. The whole point of meditation—or a practice that simulates a meditative state—is to release old, negative energies and thought patterns that might be trapped in your brain. Finding a meditative state helps to neutralize your thought patterns so that you're no longer triggered by them. Meditation is a practice. It takes time to find what works for you and to achieve that higher state. As you continue to practice daily, you'll find yourself getting more and more in the groove of it (just as with anything). Also, remember that just because you might not be seeing any results immediately doesn't mean it's not working. Think of meditation as a bank account—each time you sit down to focus on your breath, you're making a deposit. Eventually, your account will be abundant where your conscious breath will guide you through all of life's moments.

Another self-love ritual I have is what I like to call "Moi Mantras." *Moi* (as in Miss-Piggy style, French for me) Mantras are my "I love *moi*" mantras. A mantra is a sacred affirmation, often with focused detail and personal meaning, sometimes used in a devotional kind of way. Essentially, mantras are affirmations on steroids. Just like affirmations and meditation, mantras help to change your thought patterns. What you are thinking in your head is exactly what you are creating for yourself. If you are unkind to yourself, you will experience unkind experiences. Essentially, you are what you think. The great news is that your mind is completely in charge of what you think, and you can choose to take control of how you're treating yourself (which in turn raises your self-worth, self-respect, self-esteem, and of course, self-love).

When I started doing Moi Mantras, it was the next level up from my previous affirmations. I was reciting these mantras with devotion and gratitude toward myself. I stood in front of my mirror every morning, staring at my beautiful self, saying my mantras out loud. I printed them out and taped them to my bathroom mirror, sometimes saying them while doing my very mundane pattern/practice/ritual of brushing my teeth, because that was fun and humorously messy. I also printed them out and taped them to my door, putting them right in front of me each time I would leave my place, giving me no choice but to remember to think loving thoughts toward myself.

I didn't always think I was beautiful—especially first thing in the morning. Messy bedhead, no makeup, basically a hot mess. I've had all sorts of negative body-image thoughts throughout my years, especially after having been 205 pounds at one point in my life. There are still moments that I look at myself in the mirror and judge something on my body—even though I am a completely different human compared to who I was in my early twenties, mentally, physically, emotionally. When I've indulged in desserts for special occasions and my body becomes inflamed and bloated from it, I have to remind myself that it's just a temporary bloat and that I happily chose to indulge at that moment. Yet it took me years of mantras on repeat to get to the point of quickly going from body shaming to body praising. Honestly, it's something I still work on to this day.

Beyond the hot mess of being a human who just woke up from a night of rest, I was eventually able to cultivate not only acceptance of my natural state, but also adoration.

I started out with some basic affirmations such as:

- I am enough.

- I am loved.

- I am healthy.

- I am whole, perfect, and complete just the way that I am.

Eventually, once I was fully present and believed whole-heartedly in what I was affirming, I made my thoughts and words more specific, turning them into mantras.

I also began to think about what I would want my future husband saying to me. I put myself in his shoes, thinking about how he would see me, how he would express his love for me. I got specific, as specific details—especially when feelings are involved—are what help manifest the experience. I created lovely sentiments I wanted him to say to me:

- You are so incredibly beautiful when you dance around the kitchen while making us a meal.

- I love it that you know who you are, and you express your-self so freely and confidently.

- Your heart is beautiful. I love you.

I then turned these lovely sentiments into Moi Mantras:

- I am so incredibly beautiful when I dance around the kitchen making a meal.

- I love that I know who I am, and I express myself so freely and confidently.

- My heart is beautiful. I love myself.

To amp up my affirmations and mantras, I began to light a candle while reciting them. The candle represents bringing light into the intention—lighting the way, if you will. The physical act of lighting a candle adds an action to the intention and affirmation. Intention plus action equals manifestation. I created an affirmation candle line that is available on my website (heather-reinhardt.com) so that you, too, can light up your intentions. Light an affirmation candle and light up your life.

> Intention plus action equals manifestation.

At the end of this book, there are affirmation prompts for you to use. These prompts are also available on my website as a free download. Use affirmations as a tool when you are going through growth.

When you start to think higher-quality thoughts about yourself, you start to live a higher-quality life, raising up your vibration. Your experiences mirror your vibration. When your vibration is higher, your life has no choice but to match your vibration, giving you beautiful experiences. When you create ritual practices that raise your vibration, you put yourself in the position to make better choices for yourself. You naturally find yourself in better situations. When you create high vibration situations, you give yourself hope for brighter days.

> Light an affirmation candle and light up your life.

METAPHORS

I love metaphors. I love them so much that I go out of my way to make everything in life a metaphor. I use metaphors to understand things, have a comparison, and to follow my growth.

One of my favorite metaphors that I was able to relate to my life was a building that was under construction outside of my yoga studio. When the construction of this brand-new apartment building started, I had just started a writing project. While I was writing this particular project, I was also going to yoga daily to process my emotions that often came up while writing about such deep, personal experiences. I was writing about my past experiences with relationships. I was owning up to all of the things that I did that contributed to how the experiences played out, which in turn made me realize I had some self-love and self-worth work to do on myself so that my future relationship, the one with my future husband, would be the best possible experience I could co-create with him. I, myself, was under construction, rebuilding a stronger, wiser, self-loving version of myself.

I faced the building under construction while practicing yoga, so I often took notice of what was recently added to the building. I took it as a metaphor to mimic my writing and growth process—just keep adding on one thing at a time. For the building, add on a door. For my writing, add on a page. For my growth, add on another notch of self-respect. The new building was being built as I was rebuilding myself.

About nine months into my writing project, I was almost done with my hearty first draft. Just a few more little things to tweak but what I had set out to accomplish was finally starting to feel real. During that same week, I noticed that the building was almost done.

I had seen the building go from the bones of the foundational structure to almost a fully blossomed project—with all the nuts and bolts being put precisely in place to make it exactly as it needed to be a strong and sturdy building. I was able to take this metaphor and use it with my project. When you set out to accomplish something big—like starting a business, writing a novel, creating a non-profit—you have to be patiently committed to the fact that these things take time and must be done in steps just as if you were physically building a building.

I had another metaphorical epiphany while in yoga one day. While I was stable in *Ardha Chandrasana* (half moon pose), it dawned on me that my yoga practice was a metaphor for how to approach life. I had been practicing yoga almost daily for roughly three years at that time. I remembered how difficult it was when I first started practicing for me to not only get into *Ardha Chandrasana* but also to hold and expand on the pose. Regardless, every time that pose popped up in the practice, I would embrace it. Sometimes, embracing it meant falling out of it.

Finally, three years into my practice, I was able to gracefully glide into the pose and add advanced variations, fully expressing myself. It took time for me to grow into the pose, to play with my balance, to understand what happens when I try different approaches with it. During those three years, it might have appeared that I went through some trials and errors with the pose, however, it was really me learning to lay the proper foundation for it. With playful practice, I eventually learned where my hand and foot should be to create the most stability. I began to understand that if I wanted to live my best life, I had to create a stable foundation for myself (mentally, physically, and especially emotionally), which required playful practice in all aspects of life.

My favorite combination of intention, ritual, and metaphor is the experience of being a plant owner. Plants represent life quite well. When they are well taken care of, they thrive. When you forget to take care of them, they die. Taking care of any kind of plant will work, however, I used an orchid as my most recent experiment.

If you've had an orchid before, you know how fickle they can be. I was given an orchid by a friend of mine—and, sadly, all the flowers fell off within two months, even though I followed all the "how to keep an orchid alive" rules. Instead of tossing it out with the weeds, I decided I was going to rebirth it since orchids are known to go through many cycles (much like life itself).

My intention was clear: rebirth it. The ritual was to water it weekly and think happy thoughts each time I looked at it (I was literally looking at a stick... I had to get really creative with my imagination here). When it rebirthed, I used the metaphor of the new blossoms as a start to a new chapter in my life. I have successfully rebirthed this sacred orchid three times—with each time representing a new start for me.

To get any plant to bloom or re-bloom requires a consistent watering ritual, the right temperature and environment, and also patience. Just because you plant the seed doesn't mean the plant will grow overnight. The elements have to be just right—the sun, the rain . . . these things take time, they come in seasons. When you can place thoughtful intention into your experiences, create rituals that perpetuate the intentions, and learn to see your personal growth in life as metaphors, you essentially design your own version of your life, your meaningful life.

Big waves out in the ocean take time (and many, many

miles) to create. Plants take time and need the proper elements and seasons to bloom. Buildings take months to build.
If you set out to create or do something big (like the journey
of learning to love yourself), honor the time it takes to create
a strong foundation and be patient with the process. Don't
forget to watch for the signs. Signs—and metaphors—are
there to tell you that you're on the right track. Live your life
in full intention with all you do. Create rituals. Metaphor
your life more than you meme your life. You've got this.

CHAPTER EIGHT

High Vibe Tribe

Once you start doing the work to love yourself, all of your actions will create an alignment with your Higher Self (your soul). Once you become in alignment with your Higher Self, you become less willing to go back to who you used to be. This is the recognition of your self-worth. In fact, once you start to love yourself, it's impossible to go back to the life you once had.

PARTING WAYS

It's for certain you'll hear a few, "You've changed . . . " from friends and family members. Some of them will be happy for you and supportive of you on your journey. However, not everyone will be on board with your newfound self-loving lifestyle. When you begin to transform yourself and someone in your life is not transforming themselves, your paths begin to split into two different directions. The further you go on your journey of self-love, the more you'll take notice of how some people are incredibly stuck in their own chaotic infinity loop, going around and around without the awareness of having self-love. Without the awareness to notice their chaotic thoughts are creating their chaotic experiences. Without the awareness of knowing who they are at their core. Without the awareness that they hold the power in their own hands to make different choices in their lives to change their circumstances. Sometimes these people are people you once called best friends, or even siblings or parents.

It's unfortunate, but inevitable. You will outgrow some friendships when you begin to fall in love with yourself. You will grow, expand, and make new choices that better serve you—and some people you care about may stay exactly as they are. And that's okay. Everyone is entitled to their own choices of how they live their lives. Some friends may not understand you and even judge you for changing. These kinds of people want you to remain in the box they had placed you in or remain the character they have you cast as in their own movie. These people, the naysayers, are often the ones who can't get out of their own way. Don't let them be in *your* way. How they view you—and themselves—is on them.

When you love yourself and live your life making the best choices for yourself, you can spot when other people are doing the same. Just as it's inevitable that you will part ways with some people, it's also inevitable that you'll meet new people—like-minded people—who are also growing and on their own self-love journey. These people will become your new support team and you'll share your similar journeys together.

Sometimes during a self-love journey, you realize that the person you need to part ways with is your significant other. As you begin to better understand yourself and make stronger choices for yourself, you might find that you're not aligned with this person anymore. One man that was in my life toward the beginning of my self-love journey was very adamant about not wanting to have children. I, on the other hand, do want to have children. I realized that spending time with him on a dating level was a waste of my time. If I had not been on a self-love journey, I imagine I would have stuck around, fallen in love with him, all while hoping that he would change his mind. I respect myself too much to put myself through that. The self-love journey teaches you to know what you want and to do what it takes to get it, which many times means removing yourself from certain situations so that better situations can present themselves.

It's often said that we become just like the top five people we share our time with. Regardless if they're family, friends, or co-workers, become mindful of the kind of people you're spending your time with. If these five people don't share your similar views on life, then this makes them out of alignment with who you are and who you're working on becoming. Surround yourself with people who are uplifting. People who are supportive. People who love themselves—always remembering that you become just like those closest to you.

Surround yourself with people who are uplifting. People who are supportive.

So many people have control issues. I think we all do to some extent or another. I can be controlling in certain aspects of my life. Some are healthy (as in what I choose to eat and how I choose to sweat), and others can be unhealthy (as in when I want to control the outcome of situations). It's a daily practice and reminder that the only part I'm actually in control of is showing up to do my part. The rest will fall into place sans my control.

There are often people in our lives who want to control situations on our behalf, ranging from friends to family members. Parents (and sometimes siblings) especially tend to have control issues, largely due to the fact that for the first eighteen years of your life, they were in control. When you become an adult—a self-loving adult—you begin to make your own choices. Sometimes the choices you make, others may not approve of. But that's okay, because these are your choices and your life, not theirs.

Just as your thoughts are on you, the expectations that other people set on you are on them. Remember their approval of you is on them, not you. How someone else feels about you and your choices are all thoughts that they are responsible for, not yours. You just keep on making your own choices that benefit you, not them. The only expectation one can have on themselves is to grow.

When there are people in your life that remove you from your center (the ones that bring you anxiety or just generally annoy you—often family members), you have to find a way to respectfully part ways (don't ghost them). Or you have to get to a point where you're so zen that nothing they say or do bothers you. As David would say about these kinds of people, "I love you, but I don't give a fuck what you think about me and my choices."

Sometimes parting ways respectfully happens naturally. Time and distance can pull people in different directions without anyone having to ghost or have unnecessary difficult conversations. However, sometimes the difficult conversations are needed and can bring more clarity on how you can best move forward—either with them in your life or without them.

I truly believe that all people in our lives serve a purpose—even if their presence is short-lived. We can learn from every person and every lesson. If a friendship or romantic relationship dissolves, make a conscious effort to have gratitude for what you learned and experienced with said person.

When my best friend ghosted me on my birthday, my first thought was that maybe I should reach out and apologize for whatever I had done that had offended her. I spent the following week analyzing everything that had happened. I realized that I hadn't done anything. There was no reason for me to apologize. David was right—she didn't even have the courage to tell me the friendship was over or to tell me how I had offended her. She left me hanging out of her own lack of clarity. I believe the bottom line was that she departed my life because she didn't approve of the way I was living, how I was changing, how I was growing into a better version of myself. She didn't like who I had become because I represented a version of who she could become if she put in the work on herself to better her life. Yet she had no intention of actually working on herself (which was certainly her choice to make). It was easier for her to discard me since she was comfortable in the norm of repeating old patterns. At the end of the day, I was transforming my patterns into a healthier way of living and nothing was going to stop me.

When you start fully expressing and embodying self-love, people will go either one of two ways. They'll either support you on your journey, offering encouragement and sound advice, wanting the best for you (because they possess self-love, themselves). Or, they'll want you to settle and stay on their level because they're afraid of your newfound (higher) level. These people don't know how you got there, why you deserve to be there, or the work you chose to do on yourself. People are afraid of freethinking, self-loving people because people with self-love cannot be controlled, manipulated or used (people who do not love themselves often control, manipulate and use other people). It is completely okay to outgrow the people who aren't growing.

ALONE TIME

A significant part of the self-love journey is alone time. Alone time as in spending moments/hours/days without the company of others and also alone time as in not dating while working on falling in love with yourself. We all want to be with someone who loves themselves. Do you know how hard it is to love someone who doesn't love themselves? Or worse, expect them to love you when they don't know how to love themselves?

If you're already in a committed relationship and decide to work on your self-love, have a conversation with your partner about the journey you intend to take. Tell them there will be times where you'll need to curl up with a book or your journal by yourself or that you'll potentially be spending a weekend away at a yoga retreat—whatever kind of escape you need from your daily norm so you can tend to your needs during this soul-expanding time. Rally your partner as your cheerleader. Maybe they'll join you side-by-side on their own self-loving journey, where you'll grow and expand together.

If you're single, close out the dating apps for a while and take some quality time to date yourself. You have to become your own best friend and get to know every aspect of yourself. The phrase "It's not you, it's me" really rings true here. You're allowed to be a little selfish during this time period. You're growing through some massive shifts on this journey and you need to be fully focused on yourself. If you don't know how to value and respect yourself, who will? If you don't know how to love yourself the way you desire and deserve to be loved, who will? In this case, by the law of attraction, you end up with partners who also don't know how to love themselves, which is essentially the blind leading the blind. This is a recipe for disaster. If you don't know how to properly love yourself, you won't know how to properly love someone else—nor will you understand how you need to be loved.

Part of learning how to love yourself is making the choice to give yourself all that you need. Doing so takes the pressure off of other people (a.k.a. your significant other). When you meet your own needs, you take away the possibility of being disappointed when others don't (they need to be meeting *their* own needs). Then when two people who can meet their own needs come together, it's an equal and healthy partnership (both romantic partnerships and platonic friendships). When you've got a solid foundation on your self-love (your identity), then open up those dating apps and get to swiping. You'll be amazed at how quickly you can spot someone who loves themselves verses someone who doesn't, even via app. When you love yourself, you make better choices on the people you date.

I can tell you from firsthand experience that this part can and will get lonely at times. It's lonely because you are learning how to be the best company for yourself without anyone else around to entertain you. There was an uncountable number of nights during the start of my self-love journey that I would cry in the shower, admitting to the Universe that I didn't want to be alone that night. I craved intimate interaction—not just between bodies but even more so a real, meaningful connection with someone. I could have sent out a text to at least twenty different guys in my phone asking them to come over to "comfort" me, but what would that have accomplished? Adding casual sex to a situation where I was already raw would be self-sabotage, regardless of how alone I felt. I needed to learn to comfort myself, not lean on sex or someone else to do it for me, which would inevitably lead to disappointment when they wouldn't be able to "fix" me.

No one was going to clean up my emotions for me. I needed to deal with the tears and whatever emotional pain came to the surface. Emotional pain that wants to escape is not to be feared or suppressed. When we allow emotional pain to rise up out of us, this *is an act of healing*. I needed to understand the root of my emotions and how to properly deal with them on my own, healing myself from past wounds and learning how to maturely handle them if they arise again. These dark nights of the soul are where massive shifts happen. Give yourself a planted seed metaphor. You're the seed in the ground. It takes water (tears) to grow. Have the courage and grit to grow through it, sprouting your roots, knowing and trusting that the other side is where the flower will bloom. As is often said in the pop-culturized yoga world: "No mud, no lotus."

This is a sacred personal time where you get to explore things that do (and don't) work for you. So many of us have thoughts from others running through our heads. Alone in silence, you can start to decipher what thoughts are truly yours and what thoughts are not. In this quiet time, you learn to fully hear yourself, understand yourself, and heal yourself.

Recognize that you are worthy. Don't settle for less. Trust in the Universe that the absolute best options are on their way to you once you decide you're worth it—not just in relationships, but in everything life has to offer. During this sacred alone time, you'll learn about yourself. Knowing yourself—your identity—is the ultimate version of self-love. No one will ever love you as much as you can love yourself. The more you love yourself, the more someone can love you.

> **No one will ever love you as much as you can love yourself.**

ALIGNED FRIENDSHIPS

Once you've become your own best friend, you then know how to be a best friend to other people. The new friends you will attract will have a similar vibe as yours. You will inevitably create your very own **#highvibetribe**.

Once you have so intimately gotten to know—and love—yourself during Breakdowns to Breakthroughs, time spent alone, and all of the hard work you've put in to better yourself, you'll then know your boundaries while cultivating new friendships. You'll be able to know and feel immediately if someone is on your level and worthy of investing time developing a friendship. You'll know what you give and what you take, and it will be in balance with what they are giving and taking. Some of the most joyful moments of my life have been sharing time, conversations, and meaningful gifts with my high vibe tribe. I truly believe that one of the paths to genuine happiness is to give from your heart to the people you care about the most.

News flash: not everyone is meant to be your friend. Not everyone you come across will see you or understand your intentions. There's no need to personally interact with someone who is not on your level. Let them be and be an example for them. Make the strong choice to surround yourself with people who honor you like you honor yourself and will honor them.

To increase your daily dosage of positivity, remove as much negativity as you can from your life. Unfollow anyone on social media whose posts make you feel down and out or bad about yourself. Fill your newsfeed with uplifting people that are bringing light into the world. We live in a society that is overwhelmingly consumed by social media, so make sure what you're getting from the Internet is as positive as it can be. And, please don't compare your life to someone else's. Remember that what you're typically seeing from people's posts on their social media are their highlights—their reel life isn't their real life. Only compare yourself to who you were in your past to who you are now and who you are becoming. Comparing yourself to others gets you nowhere. You're not on their journey and they're not on yours—so don't waste your time, thoughts, and precious energy on comparison.

Once the friend who ghosted me on my birthday was out of my life, her departure created a space to be filled by someone else. Someone who was more aligned with my core values and also on a self-love path. Lucky me, not only did I receive one person to fill this available spot, I got a handful of absolutely wonderful women who have become my dearest friends.

The best kind of friends are the ones that can mentally stimulate you, who bring a new and fresh perspective to your life—and vice versa. For me, it can be dreadfully uncomfortable to have a conversation with someone who is a Debby Downer when I'm a Positive Petunia. Or even worse, a conversation that has zero intellectual, spiritual, and/or meaningful exchanges. I don't care about conversations about the weather; I care about if you're happy with your life choices.

I recently caught up with a friend I went to college with and it was honestly a very uncomfortable lunch. All she had to contribute to the conversation were tales of her recent shopping adventures and random pop culture happenings she'd seen on *E! News*. I acknowledge that these topics were in her comfort wheelhouse, however, I also had to acknowledge that I was not enjoying talking about nothing of importance. I find that these kinds of people have not yet tapped into their own sense of being, their own vulnerability, their own sacredness. And that's okay; everyone is on their own path.

When you know yourself, you can easily see the difference between someone who is on a self-loving path versus someone who isn't. The ones on a self-loving path are always consciously searching to be a better version of themselves than they were the day before, and they always have gratitude, whereas people who haven't quite reached self-love yet tend to lack gratitude. I aim to surround myself with people who are having deep thoughts combined with actions that help shift their world, and ultimately, our world. When one changes themselves, they change the world. These are the kinds of people I strive to know and be around as I'm able to share similar stories and gain more knowledge from someone on a similar path.

Once I had a firm grasp on my identity and began to embody the lifestyle I had worked hard to create for myself, I noticed that I was loving myself so much that I had an over-flow of love to give to others. My friends are so lucky—I spoil them to pieces! And, of course, vice versa, since the law of attraction gave me my high vibe tribe that treats me the same way that I treat them. People who have massive amounts of self-love know how to give without expectation, knowing that whatever they put out into the Universe will undeniably return to them somehow, some way in tenfold. Your ability to give a gift, your time, com-passion, along with considerate thought and conversation to someone equally mirrors your ability to give to yourself. Your ability to receive a gift is also the same mirror. When you can receive, you have an abundant mindset and are open to what life has to offer.

> **When one changes themselves, they change the world.**

Mirroring is my favorite self-reflective tool. If someone is in your life, they're serving as a mirror for you to look within yourself. If someone irks you, look in your own mirror at what is within you that is irked. It's never the other person that has irked you, rather it's a reflection of an unhealed wound that has sprung to the surface by this person's words or actions. Using mirroring helps you better understand yourself and any parts of you that may need to be healed. When you criticize or judge someone, you're only reflecting it back onto you. Become aware of your thoughts and how they reflect on you. Same goes for happier emotions. If someone makes you smile, look in your own mirror at what is within you that brings out happiness—and be grateful for it.

One of the best things that I cultivated during my self-love journey is the ability to know quickly if someone is of a similar mindset and vibration as me—not only with friends but also in dating experiences. Coming from a place of stability within myself, I was able to say no immediately to the men that I didn't have any common interests with. In the past, I said yes to every man who asked me out because I was afraid of missing out on the right guy. (Side note: the right partner never passes you by—you always end up with whom you're supposed to end up with.) I was able to step back into the dating world consciously and intuitively. If I didn't feel amazing and uplifted while first talking to a guy, why would I want to spend any of my precious and highly valued time on a date with him?

MENTORS

During your self-love journey (or really during life, period), you're going to need a friend or two that you can deeply rely on. And vice versa—be this person for them, too. There are few things greater than a mutually respected and honored friendship equal in the give and take. You're going to need someone there to talk things out with because they'll have a different perspective you won't have—but will need. Not only will you need their advice at times, you'll need them to help metaphorically push you forward to make the jump off the cliff to greatness.

I have a few friends that fill this position for me that I've mentioned throughout this book. The first two are David and Hunter. David is twenty-one years older than me while Hunter is six years younger than me—and they're both men.

I connect really well with men as I have a certain Mars energy that gives me a lot of masculine drive when it comes to creating my projects. These two men are not only mentors and close friends, but also brothers to me. They're the first ones I call when something amazing happens and also when something not-so-amazing happens. They're my team, my support system. And I, to them. They're there to offer their honest opinions and helping hands when needed. Sometimes their perspective is exactly what I need to hear to understand my own situation more. They help keep me accountable. Having a friend who helps keep you accountable is an amazing gift. To get a friend like this, you have to become a friend like this.

I also have a mentor and dear friend, Glenda, who heavily encouraged me to get on my yoga mat. She taught me by example that it's okay to shine your light brightly out into the world, regardless if other people don't see it, misunderstand it, or try hard to dim it (no one can dim your own light except you). The world needs more light. If you have it, shine it!

Cultivating your high vibe tribe starts with uplifting your own vibe. You will meet amazing people along your journey. When you shine your light, your people will find you.

CHAPTER NINE

Ebb and Flow

Life ebbs and flows. There will be great days and not-so-great days. Obstacles are unfortunately inevitable, just like the occasional head cold, tripping over your own two feet, and car accidents. Sometimes not-so-pleasant things that are out of your control happen. It's just part of life as a human. However, when you choose to embody self-love and incorporate it into all aspects of your life, your experiences—good and bad—become less autopilot and more manageable with your ability to make clearer and better choices.

This journey will have hard days. Like the old saying, "If it were easy, everyone would do it." So many people live on autopilot because it's seemingly easier to coast. But coasting can become numbing. Many people actively try to numb out the dark emotions and experiences from their past, however, that's essentially shoving it under the rug—and, that floor can get really dirty and bumpy with debris over time. Pushing down emotions and not letting them be fully expressed will make you miserable, period. If you don't experience and understand your low emotions, then it will be more difficult to grasp the gratitude of how wonderful the high emotions are. So why do people coast? It comes down to one word: *fear*.

Fear is the biggest obstacle of all as it can encompass your thoughts, patterns, and practices, essentially overtaking your entire life. There's a popular saying in many New Age spiritual teachings that is very valid: Everything is either done out of love or fear. When you make choices and take actions based on love, you set yourself up for success. You are saying to the Universe, "I trust that I will be provided with what I need and what is best for me." By the law of attraction, this mindset will bring more loving experiences to your life. When you make choices and follow them with actions based on fear, you're trying to control the uncontrollable. You're saying to the Universe, "I don't trust you or myself." By the law of attraction, this will bring more miserable experiences to your life.

I have a few friends that are in disbelief that I ever have low-vibe moments. They think I'm always upbeat and positive, never experiencing dips in energy. The main reason they think this is because when I feel a low vibe coming on, I combat it with extra doses of self-love, incorporating self-care and self-compassion. I choose to take care of myself, knowing I need more kindness and love, rather than surrounding myself with things or experiences that may be more harmful to me in this sensitive energy state.

My friends often don't see me in these phases as it's typically something I do alone. When I reemerge from my low-vibe energy cleanse, I'm back to a positive and upbeat state. I want to share with you some tips that have helped me tremendously to overcome fear, accept my vibration at all levels, and keep me balanced as I experience the ebbs and flows of life while tackling any obstacles that come my way.

INTEGRITY

Although it can be a snazzy and somewhat overused resume word, *integrity* is one of my favorite words. The general understanding is that people with integrity do what they say they'll do and are trustworthy. It seems pretty straightforward, but somehow there are so many people who lack it.

The first and foremost person you need to have integrity with is yourself. When you can align yourself with integrity, you're unstoppable. You know the person who says they are never going to go back to their ex ever again but then they get back together and repeat the same game again and again? That person is not in line with their integrity. You know the person who says they're going to start a project and end up talking about it forever without a lick of work done on said project? That person is not in line with their integrity.

Integrity is a strong choice combined with follow-through actions. To understand your own integrity, take notice of if you're able to say something and then do it. Both of these require choices—choice one is to decide to do it and choice two is to actually do it. This can be ridiculously harder than it seems. This goes right back to how you do one thing is how you do everything. If you tell someone—or yourself—that you're going to do XYZ, then never do XYZ, you're not in your integrity. When you aren't in alignment with your words and actions, you'll undoubtedly end up in a predicament. Integrity is alignment with your self-worth. When you value yourself and deem yourself worthy, you don't put yourself in situations that are out of integrity. You do what's best for you, *always*.

I used to procrastinate often, on everything. There were days that would completely slip by me where I wouldn't accomplish anything of significance. I was out of alignment with my integrity because I didn't know who I was and I didn't know what was important to me. Once I figured out what was important to me, I was able to focus on creating actions that helped me accomplish my goals, ultimately forming better habits (patterns and practices), keeping me in alignment with my integrity.

Integrity is showing up for yourself daily, doing what is best for you in all situations. It's not canceling plans, rather it's understanding yourself well enough to know to not make plans that don't serve you in the first place. It's going with what you need over what you want (what you want usually comes once what you need is taken care of). It's giving yourself the permission to close any of the doors in your life that don't work for you, which inevitably leaves the space for new and rewarding doors to swing wide open. You don't have to accept the things in your life that you're not okay with. Cut the negative nouns out of your life (negative people, places, and things).

Do yourself the ultimate favor of un-sheeping yourself.

Most people are waiting to be told what to do—being sheep—being herded along with the crowd. Do yourself the ultimate favor of un-sheeping yourself. Give yourself permission to live the life that you want to live. Then wake up every day and live it! This is integrity. You are the one holding your own key to unlock the door to your best life—so use it!

People lack integrity because they are lying to themselves (thus, lying to others). If you can't tell the truth to yourself, you certainly can't be honest with others. The truth will always set you free—especially that rock-bottom, hard truth that you've been withholding from yourself because it's difficult to pull back the horse blinders and deal with. When you have horse blinders on, you're betraying your sacredness. Be honest with yourself. Cry. Laugh. Release the shame of not being perfect (no one is!). Yell at the Universe. Do whatever you need to do to get the built-up negative energy out of you so that you can move forward with a lighter load, seeing your path more clearly.

In case you haven't guessed it by now, integrity equals self-love. Most people can grasp the concept of integrity but many struggle with the implementation of it. It can be far easier to be out of integrity than it can be to be in it, just as it can be far easier to say something than to actually do it. Your actions have to match your intentions.

When your actions don't match your intentions, this perpetuates your chaotic infinity loop. It will keep looping around and around in chaos

Your infinity loop will either keep you trapped or break you free.

until you make the choice to get very honest with yourself. You get honest with yourself by analyzing where your actions are not lining up with your intentions. When you have clarity of what actions need to be implemented to create change, the chaos of your infinity loop dissipates, leaving room for you to fill your infinity loop with self-love. Your infinity loop will either keep you trapped or break you free.

At the end of the day, we all want to look back at the choices we've made and be proud of them—even if they were choices that seemingly failed us. With each failure is a lesson needing to be learned. Learn to identify the hard lessons then become grateful for them teaching you and moving you forward on your path. They will *always* make you stronger and smarter. When you come across the inevitable obstacles of being a human, fall back on your intention with your integrity for support and guidance. Your integrity is your compass, pointing you in the direction to go.

SELF-SABOTAGE

Self-sabotage is best described as making wrong choices that can be detrimental to our growth—and, often, self-sabotage choices are made unconsciously. The most common forms of self-sabotage are procrastination and overusing substances. Procrastination is typically the product of being indecisive or having no direction. People procrastinate because they have not made a strong choice, or they are afraid to make a strong choice. However, once you make a strong choice the Universe *always* backs you up. Hunter S. Thompson put it perfectly, "A man who procrastinates in his choosing will inevitably have his choice made for him by circumstance."

You have to get clear on what you want your life to be like, then make strong choices to create that life. It's okay to take your time on getting clear, as long as it's done consciously, and not in a procrastinating way. So how *is* it done in a conscious way versus a procrastinating way? By making smaller, mindful, step-by-step choices along the way. If you're procrastinating, you have no direction. But if you're conscious, you are aware that taking steps forward, regardless of how big or small they are, creates forward progress.

Overusing substances is typically the product of wanting

to suppress your thoughts and emotions, therefore stunting your growth. I'm not talking about a glass of wine on a date with your partner or toasting champagne at a wedding—those are celebratory. Alcohol should be consumed for celebration—not coping. However, for years, unhappy members of society have turned to substances to cope, making it part of the social norm. It's not "new" news that this is killing people (physically, mentally, emotionally). To know yourself, you have to get real. Getting real means tapping into your pain. Dulling your pain with substances is self-sabotage. People want to skip out on the struggle, but that's where the gold lies.

Substance use can be a distraction from your emotional work. Drinking lowers your vibe by numbing you from fully feeling the emotional experience needed to work through your issues. There are other self-sabotaging actions that also lower your vibration—poor eating habits, poor exercise habits, spending time with negative people—pretty much anything that makes you feel depleted. These are temporary escapes from your life. Do yourself a favor and build a life you don't have to escape from. You can't run from your problems. Problems will always chase you until you dig down deep to the root of them and fix them. And you know what? Most things are just scary in the anticipation phase—once you handle it, it's not as big of a deal as you made it in your head. Give yourself the gift of allowing yourself to feel *everything* while you're growing. This includes the pain, but it also includes the joy.

When you can fully embody your integrity, self-sabotage becomes nonexistent, dissolving away as a thing of your past. I have seen so many people claim they want to start their own business but don't want to put in the work to create it. Or they don't know how to start, which is fear and procrastination (the key to anything is simply to start and go one step at a time). They choose going out for happy hour after working 9 to 5 instead of putting in the time to create their "passion." Look, if it's really your passion, you're going to choose it over everything else. If you want to create self-love in your life, your actions have to match your intentions. If not, you just keep confusingly going around and round in that chaotic infinity loop. Your own energy can't keep up with you when you say one thing and do another. You confuse yourself.

Self-sabotage is a betrayal of your sacred self, your growth. Self-love is removing yourself from harmful situations. Not only are they harmful to your physical body, but even more harmful to your energy. Acknowledge what is harmful for you, then begin to make strong choices that help remove these situations from your life.

SELF-CARE

While there are self-care maintenance routines (like my bougie baths), I also want to discuss self-care as a form of recuperation after a Breakdown to Breakthrough, or a stressful and/or emotional event. It's important to remember that when you are experiencing a low moment, this too shall pass (it always does). But when you are going through something more stressful than normal, you need to give yourself some extra self-care.

After I have a Breakdown to Breakthrough, I'm exhausted. I've usually cried (and cried hard, letting it all out) which can be downright draining. I treat myself with extra care on those days. Not only will I take a bougie bath, I'll also head to bed as soon as I can—and not just for a nap. I've had experiences where I've gotten out of my bath, closed my blinds, turned off my phone, and hopped under the covers at 4 PM, not waking till the following morning. My mind, body, and spirit need to rest and realign, so I allow it to. Sleep always resets you. It's one of my main answers to a lot of problems. Go to bed, get rest, wake up with a new perspective, start fresh tomorrow.

Another form of physical self-care I started to incorporate into my life after a traumatic event is a spa day. Spas aren't just for celebration (but, by all means, use them for that, too!); spas are a great space to recharge yourself. I was in a car accident a few years ago (thankfully, I was just a little bruised). The day after it happened, I spent five hours at a spa, hopping between the Jacuzzi, sauna, and steam room. My body needed to heal and I'm certain it did faster than normal since I created the space and situation to relax.

If my schedule doesn't allow for a day at the spa, I create a mini spa at home. I have all sorts of scrubs, oils, lotions, and so many other bottles of things that represent self-care. I recently moved, which as we all know can be a huge drain (physically, mentally, emotionally). The night before my move and also the night of my move, I spent an extra thirty minutes in my bathroom slathering on all my products, taking pristine care of myself, knowing I had put myself through a hefty transition. The least I could do was to treat myself with some extra care while going through massive change.

Reiki is also one of my favorite ways to realign my energy. I like to call it a massage for your aura. I'm also obviously a huge fan of yoga. For years, I only did Vinyasa yoga (flowing, more strenuous yoga) but when I had the car accident, I discovered Yin and Restorative yoga. My type-A personality wanted to push further but my exhausted body was like, "Nah girl, rest."

Listening to music is also a great way to realign your energy. Music is vibration so turn on something that makes you happy, let the happy musical vibrations work their magic on you.

When I'm in a lower vibration, everything feels hopeless. But when I'm in a higher vibration, everything feels hopeful. When you're low vibing, you can trick yourself into a higher vibration. I recently went through a low-vibration experience. It was the holidays and I didn't have any plans other than to rest, as my year had taken a lot out of me. I was also recovering from a cold, so my body really wouldn't let me participate in anything else other than rest. I started to feel a little pity-party energy coming through me as I saw my friends' posts with their families, opening gifts, out skiing, and doing other fun wintery things. I knew this was just a temporary feeling and that it would pass, but I decided to physically do something to trick my mind into a higher vibration.

I knew I was about to go into the upcoming year with an insane schedule. I started to view my two weeks off from work and my social life as not only a rest period but also a preparation period. I looked at my to-do list. "Clear out e-mails" had been on that list for three years (or longer). I had never made the time to sort through my 6,000-plus untended e-mails (mostly store sales and spam). I now had the time. While it was a tedious and seemingly boring task that took me nearly a week, it was a hopeful task. First, it kept my mind on something else other than my pity party of my holiday blues. Second, it cleared out unnecessary clutter. Even though it wasn't clutter in my physical space, it was still a cluttered aspect of my life. Third, I was preparing for brighter days ahead—days when my inbox would be filled with successful and joyous e-mails of everything I was creating for myself. The trick I pulled on myself worked. I had raised my vibration and was now looking forward to the future rather than being upset about where I currently was.

Maybe you need a technology break more than you need to clear your e-mails. Turn your devices off and pick up a book you've been wanting to read. Reading fiction can be a great way to consciously zone out to another world for a while, plus it can often conjure up inspiration for your next steps. Sometimes following a character on their journey can help you better understand your own journey.

When you dip low in the ebb and flow, the Universe is giving you the ultimate test to prove your self-love by how you choose to take care of yourself. You have to get to a point where you accept that this is just where you are at that said moment. Things will change, they always do. While you're in a low energy space, learn to listen to what you need. Take care of your energy. Nurture yourself. Heal yourself. When you're low vibing, do things that help raise your vibration. There will always be something else to do on your to-do list but prioritize your self-care. There are things that can wait on that list but re-aligning your energy to a higher vibration isn't one of them.

SELF-COMPASSION

You've taken a detour . . . now what? Guess what? It's completely fine. If you fall off the wagon, just hop back on again. It's your wagon, you get to steer it in any direction you choose.

As I mentioned at the beginning of this chapter, obstacles are unfortunately inevitable—we're human. It is what it is. Things happen *for* you, not *to* you. The negative things you experience are actually opportunities to grow and transmute to positive lessons. When you can adjust to that mindset, life becomes way easier in the ebb and flow of experiences and emotions.

The most important things to give yourself on your self-love journey are *self-compassion* and *patience*. Self-compassion is basically not beating the shit out of yourself when you fuck up. Self-compassion is telling yourself that it's okay and there are zero reasons to drag yourself down. Self-compassion is self-acceptance and kindness. We can be so kind to our friends, family, and even random strangers. Take some of that kindness and give it to yourself. If you're consciously taking a self-love journey, you're already doing the best you can. Don't be so hard on yourself. You've already made the choice to do the work, so cultivate patience and be kind to yourself. Patience and self-compassion are the keys to truly getting through any obstacle that life throws at you. Patience will sustain you to your next beautiful phase and self-compassion will keep you calm while you're getting there. (Side note: every stage—especially the transition stage—is a beautiful stage.)

Patience is essential on your self-love journey (or any journey, really). Change happens not in one giant step, but rather in a series of many tiny steps taken along the way. If you find yourself needing a little break, take one. Whatever break works for you—always do what works best for you.

> **Things happen *for* you, not *to* you.**

Some days I need a break from journaling. Some days I need a break from working out. Some days I need a break from my norm. Taking breaks consciously can help you find answers that you may need for the next phase. It's not procrastination when you're consciously making the choice to break and rest. When you don't know what to do, take a break. Resting for a little bit lets you recharge and refocus. When I don't know the answer to something, I take a break and remind myself that a future version of Heather will know (future Heather always figures it out).

Some days you'll get a lot done and feel great. Other days, you'll feed your dog and that's enough of an accomplishment. Life ebbs and flows. The quicker you can accept this—and cultivate self-compassion and patience during your journey—the easier it is to move through it. Self-compassion and patience help keep you from dipping to lower vibe energy by combatting your unnecessary mind-made struggles.

You'll get to your destination, that place you've worked so hard to get to. And, then you'll discover that you've got another journey in front of you. The journey of self-love is an evolution. It never actually ends, rather it continues to elevate to different levels. You graduate on to the next journey, having studied and learned (and failed) with plenty of knowledge to pave the way forward. You have to keep going (growing).

CHAPTER TEN

Courage

In today's day and age where society seemingly values superficiality, it can be downright difficult to love yourself. The world is much more set up for you to hate yourself than it is for you to love yourself. It takes massive amounts of courage to go against the grain of society. It takes massive amounts of courage to live an epic life. In fact, the journey of self-love requires you to muster every ounce of courage that you have—and then some—to move forward on your path. When you decide to go down the path of living a life filled with epic self-love, it requires all of your dedication, determination, belief in yourself, accountability, integrity, and passion. Then you have to take all these ingredients and place them into every single arena of your life. All of this takes courage!

I recently sat down with my ninety-seven-year-old grandmother. She told me I had such courage to have moved away from my home and family, across the country, to start a life with so many unknowns. People—friends, family, and strangers—have always told me I had such courage to move, but I never saw it that way. I always thought of it as not having any other option. It was my heart's calling and what was I going to do? Not follow my heart? Not an option for me.

It still shocks me that people don't follow their heart's calling. Then I remember that they are afraid and do not have the proper tools to conquer their fears and cultivate their courage. (This was the initial reason why I wanted to write and share my stories. If I can do it, so can you.) If you can think it, you can achieve it. If you're able to think it, you are fully able to go out and get it—or else the thought wouldn't have been conjured up by your mind in the first place.

Your heart's calling is what leads you to your *destiny*. Many people romanticize the word destiny. When I use the word destiny, I'm referring to what you're meant to do with your time and talents here on Earth. Fulfilling your destiny will probably make you very happy and also be a source of abundance. By the law of attraction, if you're doing what makes you happy, your energy is vibrating at a higher frequency. The Universe likes it when you're in your high vibe mode, and will provide you with abundant support (a.k.a. money) for you to keep it up. Yet society—and often, parents—will tell you the opposite; that your heart's calling (especially if it's artistic) won't pay your bills. People often fall into the fear of not being able to pay their bills and get some job (any job) that might pay their bills but puts a big damper on their heart. Or a lot of the time, people are afraid to be different, fearing judgment from others. This kind of behavior is essentially spiritual heart disease. (How many people die from heart disease? One in every four. See what I'm getting at? Follow your heart.)

If you don't know your heart's desire, destiny, or dreams,

then start actively searching high and low for all the things that make you happy. Acknowledge things that make you miserable too, since that's important to know so that you can make the choice to *not* have those things or experiences in your life. You might not have one particular calling, but a handful of callings. Something that worked for you in your twenties might not be as meaningful to you when you reach your thirties, and so on. Your tastes and desires will change as you grow and that's totally acceptable—if not downright predictable—as growth equals change. To optimize your intelligence, you must include your heart while making decisions.

To cultivate the courage to pursue your dreams, you have to come to terms with the fact that no one is going to build your life but you. You will be the reason you either succeed or do not succeed—it's up to you to make the choices that lead you on the path to your best life. Often we have resistance to moving forward. Honestly, I should have started spreading my self-love message a few years back, but I had resistance (fear) around it. I had to overcome imposter syndrome. Who am I to spread this message? I don't have a master's degree in self-love (because there is no formal education for self-love). Since there's no formal education for self-love, I had to come to terms with the fact that I had to help create an education for it via self-help, via my own stories, trials, and tribulations. I'm the woman who has read every self-help book and actively applied the lessons to my life, while continuing to learn new ones as I went along my path. With that, I became the self-love aficionado.

Feel the fear of the unknown and plow forward anyway. When you put yourself in the position where there is no other option but to follow your heart, that prompts you to be in your *courageous* energy. This energy, like all other law of attraction energy, will help you tackle the things that fear tries to block you from. Sometimes putting yourself in this position looks like quitting your job, moving to a new city, breaking up with someone (friend, romance, business, all of the above), creating a new relationship with someone. It's essentially whatever scares the bejesus out of you! Do the scary things to put yourself in courageous energy. A big choice followed by a big action gives the Universe an opportunity to conjure up a supportive response. You'll be taken care of in your courageousness.

Courage is nothing more than trusting in the Universe with an open heart. When you have trust, you know you'll always be taken care of, circumstances will manifest on your behalf that support you, and things will unfold as they should. Don't let your head do all the talking; feel what your heart wants to express to you. The two work best while in cahoots. To open your heart, you have to *feel* and *lean into it.* Do so gently, especially if you've been wounded before and closed it down. Go through all the deep and hidden emotions to open that sucker up. Warning: this is hard and may cause a Breakdown to Breakthrough, but it might be one of the worthiest things you do throughout your entire life. Peel it, feel it, heal it. **#peeltoheal**

> **Feel the fear of the unknown and plow forward anyway.**

Once it's healed, it becomes a piece of your past, no longer lingering in your present or sabotaging your future. When your heart is open, the world is your oyster. With an open heart, you become a wide-open vessel to give love and receive love (really to give anything positive and receive anything positive—but we'll use love since we've compared the two main governing forces as love and fear). The more love you put in, the more love you get out. "Get what you give" becomes far more effective when your heart is open. I use the metaphor of how one gives and receives physical gifts as a measure of how much their heart is open or closed. There's a direct correlation between how you give to yourself when you give to another. If you give gifts to people freely and with ease, you likely give yourself self-love freely and with ease.

On the other end, if you have a hard time receiving a gift from someone (or receiving a compliment or a gesture of kindness), you likely have a hard time being kind to yourself or giving yourself self-love. Giving and receiving are a balance. Our physical hearts take in blood and then give it right back out, over and over again—keeping us alive! Giving and receiving—love—is our heart's natural state. It's courageous to open up your heart. It's the way to become part of the universal flow of positive energy.

Becoming courageous takes time and a commitment to practicing and maintaining *patience.* Ahh, patience. David often reminds me that when I'm lacking patience, my courage is turned inside out. I have to sit down and realign myself to get back to my main focus, mustering up more courage (trust in the Universe) for the path—and next level—ahead.

What my grandmother didn't know was that moving was the easy part for me. Where I had to muster up my courage was when I made the choice to open up my vulnerability so that I could live my life in its fullest expression. That makes moving thousands of miles away from my home look like a walk in the park.

One courageous step is usually followed by another one, and then another one . . . and then another one:

Choosing to love and take care of myself required a new level of courage. Putting myself as a priority over everything else made me a better friend, a better team player, an overall better person.

Choosing to show up at women's networking events to share my self-love message required a new level of courage. My friend Glenda always reminds me of what her mother told her: "If you stay home, you know exactly what will happen. If you go out and meet new people, you have no clue what will happen . . . and when you have no clue what will happen, it's an adventure."

Choosing to end a relationship that had run its course required a new level of courage. We could have stayed together and forced it to work since we were genuine friends, but we would have both missed out on a better-suited partner for each of us.

Choosing to take time off from dating and consciously work on myself so that I would inevitably attract a high-quality and high vibe man with an open heart like mine required a new level of courage. (Especially when people are telling you that you're getting old and never going to meet him if you take time off from dating. Those are the kinds of people that need to be removed from your life. They clearly don't understand how energy works and are projecting their fears onto you.)

Choosing to share my stories and the message of self-love— whether through writing or speaking to large groups—requires a new level of courage. This is one fear in particular that I'll have for the rest of my life; rising up to a new level of courage each time I get on stage to speak. (Cue the butterflies.)

Choosing to plow forward after a *Breakdown to Breakthrough* requires a new level of courage.

Choosing to respect our *sacredness,* honoring our *minds, bodies,* and *spirits* requires a new level of courage.

Choosing to make *strong choices,* understanding that how you do one thing is how you do everything, requires a new level of courage.

Choosing to take *responsibility* for our own healing and every experience in our lives requires a new level of courage.

Commitment to *purpose* and the *process* requires a new level of courage.

Creating conscious *patterns and practices* requires a new level of courage.

Building *strong foundations,* setting ourselves up for success, requires a new level of courage.

Digging in and choosing to learn about the law of attraction and how *thoughts create experiences* requires a new level of courage.

Reflecting on our *inner dialogue* patterns requires a new level of courage. Then an additional level of courage to change them from negative to positive.

Forgiveness requires a new level of courage.

Becoming friends with your pain to understand it then properly heal it requires a new level of courage.

Choosing to create and understand *intentions, rituals, and metaphors* requires a new level of courage.

Parting ways with people who are not in your same vibration requires a new level of courage.

Spending *time alone* to fully understand yourself requires a new level of courage.

Creating new *high vibe tribe* friends requires a new level of courage.

Stepping into your *integrity*—and implementing follow-through from intention to action—requires a new level of courage.

Stepping out of any *self-sabotaging* behaviors requires a new level of courage.

Nurturing yourself with *self-care* and *self-compassion* requires a new level of courage.

SELF-LOVE REQUIRES COURAGE

The reason these soul-searching tasks require courage is because these things aren't usually taught in our traditional education system and can often feel a bit off the grain. Some of these things don't feel normal to us because we've never lived like this before. Now you have the chance to live in flow and harmony with the Universe. How amazing is that?

To acquire courage, "trust-fall" into the Universe. Leave all your fears at the door. Surrender into your unique journey. Show up for yourself. Believe in yourself. Create the life you want to live.

The courageous steps I just laid out are the blueprint to an epic life. As this list displays, each arena of your life demands a better version of yourself, more courage, more love, more self-compassion, more *everything* wonderful as you continue to grow.

Oh and P.S., we're all trying to figure it out as we go along. With each courageous step you take, you learn more as you go (grow).

CHAPTER ELEVEN

Amour de Soi

Amour de Soi—French, "love of self" (pronounced a-more du swa')

Live in your *amour de soi*. Be the embodiment of *amour de soi*. A life filled with self-love is an epic life. Use the tools I've shared with you in this book as you build your epic life. The foundation of building a structure starts with digging into the ground. The foundation of your self-love lifestyle starts with digging deep, reflecting on who you are. When you know and accept yourself, your deep and true identity, that's the embodiment of self-love, *amour de soi*.

OWNERSHIT

Reflection is a major key to understanding yourself and your past choices. You can't overcome and change the things that you don't fully understand. When you understand your past, you can then better understand your present experience. When you understand how you got to where you currently are, you can then course correct your thoughts, choices, and actions if needed to create a brighter future—to create the life you desire to live. Reflection work always turns into clarity. Clarity is a beautiful thing. Having clarity keeps you in your integrity and lets you know why you're doing what you're doing. The work you do on yourself today will pay off tenfold for all of your tomorrows.

Reflection work takes deep honesty with oneself. Once you get through accepting your previous choices and experiences, you can then move on to the phase of owning all the shit you've been through. I call it *ownershit*. We all have our greatest hits of the things we wish we would have done differently, and while we can't rewind time, we can *ownershit*. When you own up to all you have done—the roles you've played, the situations you've been a part of, the lies you've told (mostly to yourself), and all of the hearts you've broken (including your own)—you become free. There's nothing holding you back when you come clean to yourself—you have no one left to hide from.

Once you *ownershit*—doing the mind, body, and spirit work to come clean to your own table—you will find that you have a new perspective on life. This new perspective is often so life-changing that you then are able to discover and understand your purpose. **#ownershit**

INVEST IN YOURSELF

A few years back I did a major facelift and upgrade of my physical life, including my material possessions. It's important to note that you can be a spiritual person and still like high-quality things. I like to think of it as "metro spiritual": I meditate daily, drinking smoothies with herbs that are nearly \nounceable, all while wearing Louboutins and driving a BMW. Not all spiritual people walk around in Birken-stocks—which goes with the lesson of never judge a book by its cover. Never judge a person by what society has claimed them to be in regard to their material possessions (whether an abundance of possessions or lack thereof).

I come from a family of packrats. My grandmother has kept everything from baby clothes to Big Mac boxes (she uses them in her gardening, but still, there's an overwhelming amount of "stuff" at her house). My mom inherited her own version of a packrat but is significantly better than my grandmother. My goal was to be significantly better than my mother.

After my nine-month nomadic journey, as I was unpack-ing my things that had been in storage, I realized I didn't need half of it anymore. Things like yoga pants and T-shirts that had stains and holes in them—why was I holding on to them? They'd been in storage for nine months—it's not like I even remembered I had them or missed them.

I decided then and there that I did not want to be a woman who wore things with holes or stains on them—I am worth more than that. As I sorted through my boxes, I ended up letting go of over 200 pieces of clothing. Some I sent to my niece, some I donated, and some I just tossed because their time had come. From there on out, I made the choice to only invest in high-quality, timeless pieces.

The job I had at that time often came with gently-worn designer pieces—meaning they had been worn a few times, then given to me. My closet began to fill up with the likes of Gucci, Prada, Helmut Lang, Diane Von Furstenberg, Donna Karan, Vince, Manolo Blahnik, and Christian Louboutin. Fun fact: in 2009, I put a pair of black peep-toe Louboutins on my vision board. Six years later, they arrived in my closet.

I set the intention to have high-quality, timeless pieces and the Universe provided me with them (and, mostly free of charge—other than some slight alterations). When you physically purge things that you no longer need, you make space for other things to come in.

Around this same time period, I had also gotten a new car. I had been driving a VW Jetta that I had gotten nearly four years prior. She (her name was Jill) was new and reliable and got me around town where I needed to go. However, I knew that I wanted my next car to be a BMW. I would often get inside Jill the Jetta and picture myself already in a BMW. The power of visualization and the process of feeling like I already had it is what I believe brought me my next car.

During my nomadic adventure, one rainy morning, I was heading north on the 101 Freeway. As the traffic came to a halt in front of me, I braked just in time. However, the car behind me did not. He slammed into me, causing my car to slam into the women in front of me. My little Jill the Jetta looked like an accordion—she was completely totaled. I, however, thankfully walked away with just a few cuts and bruises.

Hunter and I went to the junkyard later that evening to retrieve a few things from the insides of Jill (by retrieve a few things, I mean we took a crowbar to the trunk to rescue my yoga mat and Prada shoes). He noticed the necklace I had on.

"Your hamsa necklace. You've had that on all day?"

I nodded yes.

He said, "Protection."

The hamsa (the hand depicted with an eye associated with Judaism and Hinduism, or as I often like to merge the two, "HindJew") represents protection. To this day, I still believe my charm of protection saved me from what could have been a really bad situation.

A few weeks later, I found myself in the showroom of Beverly Hills BMW. My nomadic experience (of not paying a hefty amount of Los Angeles rent) meant that I had a decent amount of funds saved up to get myself my dream car. So that's exactly what I did.

There are varied reasons why I drive a BMW but one of them is because I enjoy investing in myself. When you invest in yourself, you feel better, you act better, you make strong choices with ease and grace. When you invest in yourself, whether through material items, education, or therapy, you are taking care of yourself, embodying self-love. I look at purchasing my BMW as an act of self-love—it's something I had desired to attain for myself and I did. Of course, it took some time (and a few vision boards) to manifest it—and, a "protected" accident for the conditions to present themselves—but, such it is as with anything we desire in life. Manifestations take time and the right circumstances to fall into place (although I would highly advise avoiding accidents if at all possible!). I also have gratitude for my BMW because it's a physical and visual measure of how far I've come and what I've been able to create in my life. (I'm looking at you, twenty-four-year-old Heather with eight dollars in your bank account.)

INFINITY LOOP

Once you are clear from the chaotic infinity loop, you can consciously create a harmonious self-love infinity loop. Since we are made of energy and energy's natural state is to create, fill your infinity loop up with positive and beautiful energy.

This, of course, starts in your mind since your thoughts create your experiences.

I literally took pen to paper to create my self-love infinity loop. I chose words that I wanted to embody in my energy and experience: create, integrity, love, intimacy, magic, trust, grateful and happy heart. The handwritten words all intertwine in a beautiful infinity loop, now located on one of my vision boards. These words encompass my being. Take some time to meditate on the words that describe the lovely person that you already are and the lovely person you are becoming. As with everything, all of the answers are already within you and it's up to you to dig them out. I also have an infinity symbol necklace that I wear daily as a reminder that my thoughts and actions constantly create my harmonious self-love infinity loop.

I created a self-love jewelry line featuring the infinity symbol that is available on my website (heather-reinhardt.com) so that you, too, can wear as a sign of your *amour de soi*.

SELF-ISH

If you're a human, you've got struggles—maybe not all the time, but on occasion—struggles creep into all of our lives. It's just how it is on this planet. I often joke with my friends saying, "Earth is hard." Many people in the New Age community call our planet "Earth school," meaning we came here to learn and grow, which includes struggling. Self-love supports you during your struggles. Having and knowing how to use these self-love tools will help combat the low-vibe energy we inevitably all experience from time to time. When you have self-love and are low vibing, your self-love practice reminds you that it's just a phase and you'll be back to your high vibe self soon. And, as Breakdowns to Breakthroughs teach us, there's always a lesson to be learned in the low vibe, so let it play out so you can understand how to best move forward.

Self-love is the epitome of self-mastery. Self-mastery is the umbrella that encompasses self-respect, self-worth, self-care, and self-love. It's all under the same umbrella because how you do one thing is how you do everything. When you make the choice to love yourself, you make the choice to live an epic life.

Love yourself right now, exactly where you are. Love yourself now, not where you will be one day. Yes, certainly look forward to that future version of yourself and work on getting there, but love, honor, and respect where you are

Love yourself right now, exactly where you are.

right now. Change happens not in one giant step, but rather in a series of many tiny steps taken along the way. Remember this as you take the first step, and then again when you take the four-thousandth step. Change is progression. Life is progression. Keep going and keep growing.

Please do not let anyone tell you that you aren't worthy of an epic life, especially yourself. If you ever find yourself asking, "Who am I to [insert goal/dream/aspiration here]?" *Stop it.* You are valued. You are special. You came to this planet for a reason. You are sacred. The only validation you need is from yourself and in your own thoughts. When you begin to understand your own sacredness, you see that self-love is the opposite of selfish. When you embody self-love, you become *Self-Ish.*

Self-Ish is putting yourself first so that you can fill up your cup with love, then freely and lovingly let it spill out onto others. You always get what you give, so give everything out with love to receive everything in with love. Love yourself so much that it spills over onto everyone you meet. Blast the world with your worked-so-hard-for self-love. Share your self-love journey with others when they inevitably ask how you became so epic. Hopefully, it will inspire them to embark on their own journey, creating a domino effect.

Take the focus off of others (judgment, criticism, etc.) and place the focus on yourself. Digging into this deep inner work is required to save ourselves, support our struggles, and live our best lives. When you love yourself, there's no room to judge yourself. And, when you are no longer judging yourself, fully accepting yourself for who you are and the sacred path that you're on, you no longer judge others. If everyone loved themselves, this world would see peace. When you have self-love, you have love for all.

When you love yourself, there's no room to judge yourself.

Self-love is a practice and a journey. At the beginning, middle, and end of the day, self-love is all up to you. You're the one who has to live inside your own head, so fill that beautiful head of yours with kind and loving thoughts. Take care of your thoughts so that they serve you, guiding you to your best choices. Utilize your choices, remembering that you *always* have a choice. Your thoughts, choices, and actions are going to build your life—so make them the absolute best they can be so that you can **#liveyourbestlife**.

Go Love Yourself.

I AM . . .

I CAN . . .

I WILL . . .

Citations

Halcyon and On and On by Orbital (page 11). Written by Owai Barton, Paul Hartnoll, & Phil Hartnoll. Halcyon and On and On lyrics © Sony/ATV Music Publishing LLC.

The War of Art by Steven Pressfield (page 46). © Steven Pressfield, published by Black Irish Entertainment LLC.

Field of Dreams (pages 53 & 66). © Universal Studios

You Can Heal Your Life by Louise Hay (page 66). © Louise Hay, Trademark of Hay House, Inc. Published by Hay House, Inc.

The Magic by Rhonda Byrne (page 85). © Making Good LLC. Published by Atria Books.

The Lotus and the Lily by Janet Conner (page 85). © Janet Conner, published by Conari Press.

About the Author

As the Self-Love Aficionado, Heather Reinhardt really loves herself. And she wants you to really love yourself, too. Her personal belief is that self-love supports people through their struggles. Her mission is to make sure as many people as possible have the proper tools to cultivate self-love by writing and speaking about her personal stories that paved her path.

Heather launched her product line, Amour De Soi™, with the same intention: the more tools, the better. Immersed not only in writing and speaking, Heather has spent the last decade in Hollywood working in development and production, where she thrives in the creative vibes.

Next up for Heather is a fictional book series that's been adapted for television. Keep up with the latest and greatest at **www.heather-reinhardt.com.**

If you fell in [self]love with this book
and want more:

Purchase affirmation candles and self-love jewelry at
www.heather-reinhardt.com/products

Twitter and Instagram:
@heathereinhardt

Facebook community:
www.facebook.com/SelfLoveAficionado

Instagram Hashtags:
#goloveyourself   #goloveyourselfbook
#liveyourbestlife   #ownershit   #peeltoheal
#highvibetribe   #amourdesoi

Heather is available for speaking engagements,
panels, radio & podcast interviews, magazine
interviews, TV appearances, hosting, along
with other media opportunities.

To book Heather, please email
info@heather-reinhardt.com.